SELLING WOMEN SHORT

Also by Liza Featherstone

Students Against Sweatshops

SELLING WOMEN SHORT

THE LANDMARK BATTLE FOR WORKERS' RIGHTS AT WAL-MART

LIZA FEATHERSTONE

BASIC
BOOKS

A Member of the Perseus Books Group
New York

Books published by Basic Books are available at special discounts for
bulk purchases in the United States by corporations, institutions, and
other organizations. For more information, please contact the Special
Markets Department at the Perseus Books Group, 11 Cambridge Center,
Cambridge MA 02142, or call (617) 252-5298 or (800) 255-1514, or e-mail
special.markets@perseusbooks.com.

Designed by Lisa Kreinbrink

Library of Congress Cataloging-in-Publication Data

Selling women short : the landmark battle for workers' rights at Wal-Mart /
Liza Featherstone.
    p. cm.
    Includes bibliographical references and index.
    ISBN 0-465-02315-0 (alk. paper)
    1. Sex discrimination in employment—United States. 2. Sex
discrimination in employment—Law and legislation—United States.
3. Sex discrimination against women—United States. 4. Wal-Mart (Firm)—
Trials, litigation, etc. 5. Industrial relations—United States—Case studies.
I. Title.

HD6060.5.U5F4 2004
331.4'133'0973—dc22

                                                        2004010298

04   05   06 / 10   9   8   7   6   5   4   3   2   1

Contents

INTRODUCTION:
AMERICAN GOLIATH

"IT'S NOT EASY to have a family and a career," says the woman in the commercial earnestly. "But my company makes it a lot easier. My company takes family very seriously." The woman, "Margaret," is shown at home, spending relaxed quality time with her husband and children.

Beginning in mid-2003, American TV viewers were bombarded with advertisements like this one from a surprising source: Wal-Mart. The commercials were light on details—Margaret, a district manager for the retail chain, never says what Wal-Mart does, exactly, to help her balance motherhood with her demanding job—but their tone was inspiringly upbeat. In a similar ad, a middle-aged black woman talks about her successful career as a Wal-Mart department manager, smilingly pronouncing it a company of great "opportunity" for women. The woman says she is so pleased with her Wal-Mart career that she urged her daughter to apply for a job with the company. Now, both mother and daughter are enthusiastic members of the "Wal-Mart family."

Had the nation's favorite retailer shed its famously conservative, music-censoring image and embraced a women's-
rights agenda? Not yet. These ads were part of a concerted
attempt by the company to stave off a public relations disas-
ter personified by a woman who looks a little like the happy,
nameless department manager in the commercial but whose
experience working for Wal-Mart was exactly the opposite.

That woman was Betty Dukes, a 54-year-old Wal-Mart
worker in Pittsburg, California. Like her TV counterpart, she
is African American, and she came to Wal-Mart hoping to
get ahead. First hired by the company in 1994 as a $5-per-
hour part-time cashier, Dukes was an eager employee with
a sincere admiration for the "visionary spirit" of the chain's
founder, Sam Walton. A year later, with excellent performance reviews, she was given a merit pay raise and a full-time
job. Two years later, after being promoted to the position of
customer-service manager—an hourly, not salaried, position, despite the "manager" designation—she began en-
countering harsh discrimination from her superiors: she was,
she says, denied the training she needed in order to advance
further; meanwhile, that training was given to male employees, many of whom were younger than Dukes and newer to
the company.

When Dukes complained about this discrimination, managers got back at her by writing her up for minor offenses
like returning late from breaks—offenses routinely committed by her white and male coworkers for which they were
never punished, she says. When she kept complaining, she
was denied a promotion and finally was demoted back to her

cashier job. She went to the Wal-Mart district office to complain, but the company did nothing. Not only was the demotion humiliating, but the cashier job offered fewer hours and lower hourly pay, and being demoted disqualified Dukes from other promotions—a worker who has recently been disciplined can't be promoted. Even when she was once again eligible for promotion, four new management positions were filled by men. They hadn't been posted, which meant that other women besides Dukes were sidelined.

Before working for Wal-Mart, Dukes didn't know the meaning of the term "sex discrimination." She had long assumed it referred to something sexual—"like Bill Clinton, or Anita Hill"—and as a woman of traditional morality, figured it had nothing to do with her. "As a single person, I don't think much about sex or sexual activity," she explains.[1] "I didn't want to go around hollering 'sex'!" Of her treatment at Wal-Mart, she says, "I knew it was unfair." Until she heard that other women were bringing a lawsuit against the company, however, she didn't know it was illegal. She suspects she's not alone in her lack of sophistication about this issue: "A lot of women are being sex-discriminated against every day and don't know it."

Dukes, who still works full-time for Wal-Mart, is now a greeter rather than a cashier, which is not a promotion. "Greeters," as every Wal-Mart shopper knows, are the cheerful, friendly people—usually seniors—who welcome you as you walk in the door and, as you leave, thank you for shopping at Wal-Mart. Dukes's wages are still so low that in addition to her full-time Wal-Mart job she has had to take a second job working as a part-time house cleaner and companion to an elderly woman in exchange for rent. Without that arrangement Dukes would be unable to get by, even though she has no dependents and spends most of her free time in her Baptist church, where she is an associate minister.

In late spring 2000, Dukes filed a claim against the company. She soon learned that her experiences were not unique; they were shared by women all over the country. The following year she became the lead plaintiff in *Dukes v. Wal-Mart Stores, Inc.,* a would-be class-action suit representing 1.6 million women who are past and present employees of the company. Filed in the U.S. District Court in San Francisco in June 2001, the suit charges Wal-Mart with discriminating against women in promotions, pay, and job assignments, in violation of Title VII of the 1964 Civil Rights Act, which protects workers from discrimination on the basis of sex, race, religion, or national origin. Plaintiffs' attorneys filed a motion for class certification on April 28, 2003. Wal-Mart's guilt or innocence was not at issue at that stage. The question was, would the judge find enough evidence of possible systematic discrimination for the case to proceed as a class action. On June 22, 2004, the answer was a resounding yes: the judge certified the class, and *Dukes v. Wal-Mart* became the largest civil rights class-action suit in history.

Wal-Mart officials, concerned, they said, that their answers could affect the *Dukes* litigation, declined to answer questions for this book. "We wouldn't be able to comment until it's all over," said Christi Gallagher, one of Wal-Mart's ever-gracious spokeswomen. (Like Wal-Mart employees at all levels, people in the corporate headquarters in Bentonville, Arkansas, are friendly and polite.) Wal-Mart is, at this writing, hoping the certification decision will be reversed on appeal.

Dukes uses a story from Scripture to explain her case to fellow churchgoers, who are mostly elderly and black. "They understand David and Goliath," she says. "I tell them, *Betty Dukes v. Wal-Mart* is like David versus Goliath." Indeed, the Biblical David could never have anticipated such a Goliath. It topped the Fortune 500 in both 2002 and 2003, and is the world's largest retailer. Its sales totaled $244.5 billion in fiscal year ending in January 2003, a 12 percent increase over the previous year. More than twice the size of its largest competitor, Home Depot, Wal-Mart dominates the retail sector overwhelmingly.

From its beginnings in Rogers, Arkansas, in 1962, Wal-Mart has burgeoned to 3,500 Wal-Mart stores in the United States—general merchandise stores, Wal-Mart Supercenters, smaller stores called Neighborhood Markets that are one-fourth the size of the Superstores, and stores in Sam's Club, a membership warehouse chain named after Sam Walton. Most of the company's growth is in Supercenters, which are open 24 hours a day and offer a full line of groceries. The Supercenters are like supersized supermarkets, covering up to 260,000 feet of store space and employing as many as 550 workers. In the United States, 41 Supercenters opened in January 2004 alone, up from a mere 14 the previous January. But this is not the only focus of expansion: the company has also developed smaller stores called Neighborhood Markets, which are one-fourth the size of Supercenters. Wal-Mart has stores in every state of the union and also operates more than

1,100 stores outside the United States—in Mexico, Puerto Rico, the United Kingdom, Canada, Argentina, Brazil, China, South Korea and Germany. Every week, more than 138 million people shop at Wal-Mart.

Wal-Mart has completely transformed the retail industry with a single-minded focus on giving the customer the lowest possible price. Many other retailers have imitated its formula—Circuit City, Dollar General, K Mart, Toys R Us, Staples, Blockbuster, Rite-Aid, Home Depot, and numerous others. Wal-Mart is important not only because of its own success but also because it drives down competitors' and suppliers' prices. The journalist Bob Ortega observed in his book, *In Sam We Trust: The Untold Story of Sam Walton and Wal-Mart,* that Wal-Mart's "way of thinking. . . has become the norm," not just in retail, but in all businesses.[2]

As of March 2004, nearly 2,600 American towns and cities have at least one Wal-Mart or Sam's Club. The company is growing so fast that many analysts expect it to run afoul of antitrust laws by 2009. Recently, its growth has been virtually unabated by a slow U.S. economy; with unemployment rates high and wages slack, people badly need the discounts Wal-Mart offers.

From the Third World factories in which Wal-Mart's cheap products are made to the floor of your local Wal-Mart where they're displayed and sold, it is women who bear the brunt of the company's low prices. With more than 1.2 million workers in the United States, Wal-Mart is the nation's largest private employer, and the majority of Wal-Mart's "associates" (the company's treacly euphemism for employees) are women. Women make up 72 percent of Wal-Mart's hourly workforce (nonsalaried workers), but only 34 percent of its managers are women. Women also earn less than their male counterparts in nearly every position at the company. According to an economist hired by the *Dukes* plaintiffs to analyze the data, these patterns do not vary dramatically by region, and have remained fairly consistent over time.

Indeed, Wal-Mart seems in many ways virtually untouched by the women's movement of the 1970s, and by the substantial progress women have made in recent decades toward greater social and economic equality. "I burned my bra, for Christ's sake! We should be past this," says Kathleen Mac-Donald, now 47, with a sigh. She is a witness in *Dukes* who works as a sales clerk in an Aiken, South Carolina, Wal-Mart. "We should be past the gender discrimination and women's rights and civil rights. This should all be in the past." Mac-Donald says she had assumed women were making progress in America. "We won the right to vote. We were being accepted. Women were leaving the home front and going to work." But from the way Wal-Mart treats women, she says, relishing her polemical style, "we might as well be in Afghanistan."

Dukes v. Wal-Mart Stores, Inc., now has six named plaintiffs who represent a larger class who agree to be its public face and to act in the interest of the group. In addition to these six plaintiffs there are more than 100 "class member witnesses"—current and former Wal-Mart workers in over 30 states who support the *Dukes* motion for class certification and have provided sworn affidavits in which they tell stories similar to Dukes's.

I researched and wrote this book between October 2001 and April 2004, after Dukes filed her suit and the plaintiffs announced their intention to seek class-action status. During much of that time, both sides engaged in discovery—or evidence gathering—to prepare their arguments for and against class certification, compelling each other to surrender telling documents, hiring expert witnesses with opposing interpretations of Wal-Mart's employee data, and questioning witnesses. In depositions taken in law offices around the country, plaintiffs' lawyers deposed Wal-Mart store managers and corporate officials, while Wal-Mart deposed the plaintiffs and many of the class-member witnesses supporting them. Plaintiffs' lawyers were able to get access to internal memos, reports, and minutes of meetings, all of which helped them to build a case that Wal-Mart was responsible at the corporate level for sex-discriminatory policies and practices in its stores. *Selling Women Short* is based primarily on interviews with *Dukes* plaintiffs, witnesses, and lawyers, as well as both sides' experts' reports and transcripts of depositions (I was not allowed to be present at depositions.)

If *Dukes v. Wal-Mart* goes to trial, it's unlikely to be resolved in less than five years. It is unclear whether there will be a trial: in class-action suits, both parties often decide to settle. But because of its scale, and Wal-Mart's importance in the national economy and culture, *Dukes* is of great public interest even if it never goes to trial.

Dukes takes place against a backdrop of bad job opportunities for poor and working-class women, who can no longer fall back on welfare if they leave bad jobs, or choose to stay home with their children. They are historically shut out of better-paying, unionized blue-collar jobs like plumbing and construction. Nationwide, through relentless cost cutting, retailers like Wal-Mart are driving down wages and benefits for women, who make up the majority of their employees. Advocates of harsher welfare policy have often touted "work" as a simple cure for poverty, but the fact is that large numbers of women leaving the welfare rolls have nowhere to go for employment but retail sales, and many end up at Wal-Mart; there, they face not only low wages but unchecked sex discrimination. *Dukes v. Wal-Mart* represents the first systematic attempt to redress this problem.

In February 2004, Wal-Mart was named *Fortune* magazine's "Most Admired Company" for the second year in a row. Indeed, Wall Street loves the company, and the rest of the business world is in awe of its profits, which increased 14 percent from fiscal year 2002 to 2003. The headline of a 2003 *Business Week* story was "How Wal-Mart Keeps Getting It Right."

But *Dukes v. Wal-Mart* contributes to a new—and impassioned—public debate over Wal-Mart. Many people are realizing that Wal-Mart is a scandal, not a praiseworthy business model: its profits and low prices come at a terrible human cost. Sex discrimination is not Wal-Mart's only crime against its employees. Workers who make clothing and toys sold at Wal-Mart, mainly young women in Asia, labor under dangerous conditions for very low pay and are treated considerably worse than employees in the United States. Ten percent of all goods imported to the United States from China are sold at Wal-Mart; in China, where the company operates 35 stores with 18,000 employees, independent trade unions are illegal, and it is almost impossible for human rights groups and American companies to monitor factory conditions. But Wal-Mart makes the conditions much worse than they need to be, pressuring factory bosses to cut their prices, so those bosses have no choice but to make employees work longer hours for lower pay. If Wal-Mart were a country, it would be China's fifth-largest export market.[3]

Wal-Mart probably wishes all countries were just like China, with no meaningful labor laws (in fact, in March 2004 the company announced that it would for the first time hold its board of directors' meeting in China[4]). Here in the United States, the company is notorious for ignoring federal laws protecting workers' rights. Wal-Mart has little respect for freedom of association, and has been found guilty of retaliating against and even firing workers for union organizing. Wal-Mart has also been accused, in class-action suits filed in more than 30 states, of breaking federal overtime laws by forcing employees to work off the clock. In many cases, workers say, managers locked the store doors and would not allow employees to leave. "If you objected you were put in your place real fast," says Lorraine Hill, who worked for Wal-Mart in Rock Springs, Wyoming. "They'd say, 'Do you want this job or not?'" Hill says workers were told to punch out and keep working. Managers would stand by the locked doors and make sure employees didn't leave. This happened, says Hill, "almost every day."

Sometimes, contrary to official company policy, there was no manager with a key on duty. In a few instances, workers who had been forbidden under any circumstances to use the fire exit for anything but a fire faced agonizing dilemmas over what to do when seriously injured.

In October 2003, a raid by federal agents revealed that Wal-Mart was hiring thousands of undocumented immigrants as janitors, many of whom have said they were forced to work seven days a week with no time off. A civil rights suit and a potential civil rights class-action suit charges that officials at the highest levels of Wal-Mart management conspired to violate federal laws protecting the immigrant janitors' rights or at the least knew about the practice. Wal-Mart became a national laughingstock. But, as Jon Stewart, the host of Comedy Central's *The Daily Show* observed, the company's policies could hardly come as a surprise. Stewart played a clip of a customer loading up her car with groceries in a Wal-Mart parking lot who earnestly declared herself "shocked" by the allegations. "You're shocked?" Stewart exploded. "Lady, you just bought a sweater for ninety-nine cents! Something's got to give!"

Amid such ongoing embarrassments, the company is starting to look much worse than Enron. Both companies are grim symbols of the greedy pursuit of profits at the expense of human beings, including their own employees. The corporate malfeasance at Enron is no longer making headlines, but many workers are hoping Wal-Mart's crimes won't be so quickly forgotten.

Betty Dukes, for her part, wants to let the public know about Wal-Mart's wrongdoing, including the dishonesty in its commercials, especially those featuring black women. She hopes to put a stop to it by forcing the company to live up to its promises. "I want to work for the Wal-Mart on the TV," she laughs. "Because it's the real world when you get to my store, and it's hell on wheels!"

1

FEMALE TROUBLE

THE STORY OF *Dukes v. Wal-Mart Stores, Inc.,* begins not with Betty Dukes but with a white Texan woman Dukes's junior by more than two decades. Stephanie Odle began working at Sam's Club in November 1991 in Lubbock, Texas (home of the 1950s rocker Buddy Holly), shortly after the Lubbock club opened. Stephanie's father heard that Sam's Club, Wal-Mart's wholesale merchandise division, was a good place to work, and he urged her to put in an application. Odle, who was 20 at the time, had graduated from Lubbock High School and studied briefly at the local community college before dropping out. She had also worked in various positions at McDonald's—as a counter person, at the drive-through, and at the grill—and had worked her way up to lead shift manager. She had to quit that job when she dropped a helium tank on her foot and could no longer stand for long periods of time. Then she became a Sam's Club "demo girl," a job for which only women are hired, handing out free samples of food to customers at $6 an hour. The job began as a part-time seasonal position—she worked at Toys R Us at the same time—but eventually she became a full-time cashier. Odle, now 32, still remembers how much she loved Sam's Club when she started: "I wanted to work my way up the ladder—and I just knew this was the company I wanted to be with forever. I didn't have any desire to work anywhere else. I felt I had a home at Sam's Club. Sam Walton was my hero," she continues. "My first impressions of the company were just absolutely awesome."

She wore a pin decorated with Walton's face to show "how much I stood for him and believed in him and the company." Like many Wal-Mart workers, Odle was deeply inspired by Walton, who had built his retail empire from humble beginnings, and she took seriously the company's promises that hard work could pay off. She became such a paragon of company spirit that she was selected to teach Sam Walton's principles to her coworkers in optional "Strive for Excellence" classes. "I was just helping Wal-Mart-ize the rest of the company, I guess," she says now. "It gave me great pride to work for them and be part of their family, the Wal-Mart family."

Odle would end up working in 11 different Sam's Clubs in three states. She transferred to a Dallas club in 1992, when she and her older brother tired of small-town life and he wanted to move together to a bigger city. There, bored with working as a cashier and itching with ambition, she wrote on her evaluations, in the space for "Associate's Comments," that she wanted to move up in the company, and was excited about the opportunities Sam's Club offered. But nothing happened: she remained a cashier.

During a year-long, unhappy marriage to a s erviceman in the U.S. Marines, Odle transferred to California and, in 1994, after leaving him, was promoted into the assistant-manager training program, which she completed success-fully. Much is asked of assistant managers at Wal-Mart, both men and women. Stephanie Odle says she worked about 70—sometimes 80—hours a week, and other current and former managers say that's typical. She has testified:

> I gave them everything they asked for, and more. I gave every-thing I had. . . . I never balked at being called in the middle of the night to go check on an alarm. I gave up lunch hours, weekends, vacation time, and holidays to be there when Sam's Club needed me. I got on a plane and flew home after work on Christmas Eve, then got on another plane and flew back before dinner on Christmas Day, not just once—every year.

One summer day in 1996, working as an assistant manager at the Riverside, California, Sam's Club, a routine moment of confusion dramatically changed Odle's view of the com-pany. An hourly worker handed her a piece of paper that someone had left in the receiving office. Odle glanced at it quickly, distracted with the day's many tasks. It was a W–2 form belonging to a coworker, Mario Arenales, like her an assistant manager. Odle was about to put it somewhere safe, so she could remember to give it back to him. But a few numbers caught her eye, and she stared at the tax form in disbelief. Arenales was making $10,000 a year more than she was. She felt as if she'd been punched in the stomach.

Not only did she and Arenales do the same job, it was also his first year with Sam's Club. Odle had been there for more than five years. Arenales had come from AutoZone, a national car repair chain, and "he didn't have any of our culture, any Big Box experience," says Odle, still indignant. "And I'd been with the company since 1991."

Odle complained about the disparity to the district director of operations, Phil Goodwin, who told her, "Mario supports his wife and his two kids." Goodwin, who knew Odle was pregnant, and about to become, like many Wal-Mart workers, a single mother, then humiliated Odle by requiring her to provide him with her personal household budget so he could decide whether or not she deserved to be paid as much as her coworker. Odle obliged Goodwin, itemizing her credit cards, rent, utilities, car and insurance payments, and projected childcare expenses. ("Then that's depressing," she recalled wryly, "when you find out you really *don't* make enough money.") "At the time," she says, explaining her acquiescence, "you have to remember that he presented this to me like, "I am doing you a favor. Give this budget to me, and I will work my hardest for you.' And I didn't think. I was, like, 'Okay, great. Thanks!'"

After submitting to this mortifying ritual, Odle got a raise of $40 per week, which didn't bring her salary even close to Mario Arenales'. "It was nothing," she says now. But her reaction at the time was a divided one: she really wanted to believe the company she loved was doing the right thing, yet the situation didn't seem fair. "One half of [my] mind, I'm like, 'Wow, these guys really helped me out,' and the other half, I'm thinking, 'What?!'"

Over the next three years, Odle was transferred four more times and endured numerous painfully sexist incidents. Working in Sherman, Texas, she and Stephanie Selinger, a female general manager, conceived an idea to save the store millions of dollars a year. One of the most successful aspects of Wal-Mart's culture is its ability to make associates feel as if they have a stake in the company, despite its vast profits and their low wages. One of these gimmicks is the "Bright Idea"—part of an initiative called "Yes I Can, Sam," which solicits workers' ideas for improving the company ("improving" in this context always means saving money).

Odle and Selinger, after reviewing nightly sales of the Tire and Lube Express and comparing them with the number of people on duty, found that keeping the tire shop open until 8:30 P.M. "was a waste of payroll. It didn't pay for itself," Odle remembers. Odle and Selinger recommended closing the tire shop half an hour earlier every day. The district manager dismissed the women's suggestion, telling them flatly that it was out of the question. A few months later, Odle's new area manager, a man, told her, "Starting next week, I want you to close the tire shop at eight." Odle was surprised, and explained that she and Selinger had made this suggestion just a few months earlier, and had been firmly rejected. He shrugged, "Guess it's a man thing. Close the tire shop next week at eight."

Odle and Selinger had submitted their tire-shop proposal in the "Bright Idea" spirit. When the idea was first rejected, Odle would testify in a *Dukes* deposition years later, "I just wrote it off as a not-so-bright idea. Then all of a sudden it became somebody else's, a man's Bright Idea, and got accepted."

Still, she was given some hope of advancement. While she was in Sherman, the regional director told her she would soon be promoted to the job of comanager of a Tulsa, Oklahoma, Sam's Club—"a big promotion, a huge raise for me," Odle recalls. "I had some friends in Tulsa who even called and said, 'Hey, they told us we're getting a girl from Sherman, Texas! That's you.'"

Soon afterward, a man from a Florida Sam's Club wanted to move to Tulsa. Odle was disciplined on a cash register technicality, and denied the promotion to Tulsa—to make room for this man, she believes. "Everybody had already told me I had the job," she says. "Then they just decide, 'Hmm, this guy's more important than you are.'"

Just after denying her this promotion, Odle's managers compounded the insult by transferring her back to Lubbock, the small hometown she'd hoped to escape by working for a huge multinational company. A few days after receiving this devastating news, Odle went to the emergency room with chest and stomach pain. "I was throwing up," she recalls. "In the middle of the night, I couldn't breathe. I just had these horrible pains in my chest. My heart hurt. I just felt like everything was tight. I had to lay down on the ground and put my hands behind me, just stretch out as far as I could to be able to breathe right." At the hospital, she was given anti-anxiety medicine. A doctor there found she had gallstones related to extreme stress. She had to have her gallbladder removed and take a 90-day leave of absence.

Even though Sam's Club was destroying her mental and physical health, and she wasn't thrilled to be back in Lubbock, Odle went back to work with a good attitude. She'd begun her Sam's Club career at the Lubbock club, and had fond memories of it, despite the discrimination and disrespect she'd experienced. She recalls telling herself, "It's okay. This is your career. This is what you love. That whole experience was just bad and we're just going to put it all behind us, go forward, be happy."

And for a while, it looked like Lubbock might work out that way. "In four months I got us on TV three times, as the marketing manager," she boasts proudly. "We had football, basketball, volleyball players come out and sign balls for Literacy Day, and we got great coverage. Everything was so positive."

That October, Odle was denied the opportunity to take a skills assessment test, which determines an employee's strengths and weaknesses and provides crucial data for future promotion, yet three male colleagues were allowed to take it. When she told her supervisor she wanted to take the test, too, he told her he only had three copies. Odle recalls, "I was like, 'What? Make another copy!' I mean, isn't that the lamest excuse ever?" She demanded to know why the three men were allowed to take it and she was not. She never got a good answer.

Later that month Odle was training hourly workers on a new checkout procedure. In the course of the training exercise they mistakenly introduced a $13.74 cash register discrepancy. Odle immediately explained the discrepancy to the accounting department and the store manager, and they were untroubled by the incident. Two days later she was fired, supposedly over the missing $13.74. Management's real reason for firing her, she charges, was retaliation for her complaints about discrimination and to make room, once again, for a man who wanted her job. Later, she remembered overhearing the store manager on the phone with a friend of his, a man from an Arizona Sam's Club who wanted to move to Texas. "Don't worry," the manager had said, just two weeks before Odle's firing. "Larry will make room for you." She learned that the man had left his Arizona job the day before her supposed violation. This man no longer works for the company. Odle, who had planned to devote her life to Sam's Club, was casually replaced by a man who now works at Hobby Lobby.

Odle filed a sex discrimination claim with the Equal Employment Opportunity Commission (EEOC) on October 22, 1999. After that she was rehired for a few days, and then she was fired again, this time, she charges, in retaliation for her complaint with the EEOC. "The men of Sam's Club left me, a single mother of a two-year-old child, with no income and no health insurance," Odle has testified. It was a month before her daughter Sydney's birthday, and two months before Christmas. "Then, to prove that Sam Walton was really dead," she says, "they challenged my claim for unemployment benefits."

After she was fired, Odle was a wreck. "I was so distraught, I was so emotionally gone." As if to apologize for bringing up something so "trivial," she says, "Not that this mattered, but I gained twenty pounds in thirty days. I couldn't get out of bed. I couldn't get dressed." Before long, though, she realized she had to set her young daughter a better example. "I had a little baby, and she's looking at me every day, and I'm saying, "Okay, you know what? She is not gonna go through what I have gone through. I refuse. These people are going to change, and I am gonna make them change, and I don't care what I have to do."

She called every lawyer she'd ever heard of, including Johnnie Cochran. She drove 350 miles to Dallas to meet with a few, including one Irene Jackson, who charged her $150 only to tell her, "You do not want to take on Wal-Mart." Most women who have sought to sue Wal-Mart have been similarly discouraged, as few small firms have the resources to fight the company.

Odle's mother, Paula, was determined that her daughter be treated fairly and encouraged her to keep looking. Surfing the Internet, Paula found Stephen Tinkler, a New Mexico lawyer who had won substantial settlements in sexual harassment suits against Wal-Mart. With his partner, Merit Bennett, he'd also litigated about a hundred civil claims of sexual abuse against the New Mexico Catholic archdiocese, years before similar scandals erupted in Boston. Stephanie laughs. "My mother said, 'This man Stephen has the guts to depose the archbishop—he's the one!'"

In the course of bringing sexual harassment suits against Wal-Mart, Tinkler and Bennett had learned a great deal about the company, which as late as the mid–1990s had no effective sexual harassment policy. "It was our theory," Tinkler explains, "that if you don't have a good sexual harassment policy, and if you don't stop sexual harassment, then there is probably a lot more going on than just harassment. Probably there is pervasive sexual discrimination." Following that intuition when litigating one harassment case, Tinkler and Bennett were able to compel Wal-Mart to disclose personnel data revealing shockingly few women in management positions. The statistics had resulted in a quick settlement of the harassment case, and several million dollars for the plaintiff. It was clear that Wal-Mart knew it had a huge sex discrimination problem and had done nothing about it for many years. Years before Odle contacted them, the New Mexico lawyers had realized that the Bentonville behemoth contained the potential for an enormous class-action suit, and they began keeping their eyes open for a plaintiff.

In 1998, a call came in from a store manager in a Santa Fe Wal-Mart who had been fired after complaining about sex discrimination. Tinkler and Bennett knew a jury would be impressed that she had advanced so far within the company and still was experiencing discrimination. "We thought she was the one," recalls Tinkler. But as most people do, the woman grew frightened of taking on Wal-Mart, backed down, and returned to her hometown in Arkansas. Tinkler recalls, "She felt intimidated, and decided she didn't want to [sue] at all, not individually or as a class action. . . which is totally understandable."

When Stephanie Odle came to Tinkler and Bennett's offices nearly two years later, they were struck by her determination, courage, and devastating case against Wal-Mart.

Tinkler recalls, "We told her we had some confidential information that led us to believe she was not the only one." They asked her if she'd be interested in becoming a representative in a national class action.

If Odle had sued Wal-Mart on her own, represented by such Wal-Mart–savvy attorneys as Tinkler and Bennett, she'd likely have won a substantial settlement within a couple years. If, on the other hand, she became a plaintiff in a large class-action suit she wouldn't see any money for years—if ever—but if the suit succeeded, Wal-Mart could be forever transformed. Odle didn't hesitate; her original idealism about the company has given way to a passion for changing it: "I don't care about anything else other than making these people do what's right," she says.

Yet because of its potentially enormous scope, and Wal-Mart's daunting resources, Odle's was not a case Tinkler and Bennett's small firm could take on alone. Just to get some advice, Stephen Tinkler called Brad Seligman, a civil rights lawyer based in Berkeley, California, with 21 years' experience in class-action litigation. Seligman and another attorney, Guy Saperstein, then partners in the Oakland firm Saperstein, Seligman, Mayeda & Larkin, had in 1992 won a $170 million settlement award for the plaintiffs in *Krasewski v. State Farm*, a sex discrimination class-action suit in which employees accused the company of refusing to hire women as insurance agents. The plaintiffs' lawyers got $70 million for their time, plus a $30 million contingency fee (meaning the attorneys' previously agreed upon portion of the settlement).[1] The same year, Seligman and Saperstein also won a substantial settlement in *Stender v. Lucky Stores*. As these cases were resolving, each lawyer retired from his partnership in the firm.

Saperstein embraced his wealth with gusto, as most people expect plaintiffs' lawyers to do. He bought a mansion in Piedmont, an affluent Oakland neighborhood. The house is so big that it has a pond in its front yard: indeed, shortly after he bought the house, under the headline "Rich Guy Saperstein," the cover of *California Lawyer* magazine showed him kayaking in his pond. Seligman, by contrast, felt that it was "embarrassing for an old revolutionary to have that much money."[2] In late 1992, he used his earnings from *Stender v. Lucky* and *Krasewski v. State Farm* to start the Impact Fund, a foundation that would help smaller firms and nonprofits litigate large-scale cases with significant social implications.[3] He saw that a conservative backlash against class-action suits whereby companies were falsely characterized as the helpless victims of increasingly frivolous lawsuits, together with the growing power of huge corporations, were making it increasingly difficult for little people to sue big capital.

The Impact Fund's modern office, flooded with natural light, is located in a beautiful office park overlooking the quiet Berkeley Marina. The Berkeley lawyer was intrigued by Stephanie Odle's potential class action. A lawsuit challenging the nation's largest employer was perfectly suited to the Impact Fund's mission, as well as to Seligman's particular body of experience litigating on behalf of low-wage retail workers. He had brought over 40 civil rights class actions—and the settlement in *Stender v. Lucky Stores* had been the third largest of its kind.

Seligman began to research Wal-Mart, hoping to find out how strong the New Mexico lawyers' case was. Since Tinkler and Bennett had obtained their damning data under a confidential court order, they couldn't use it to bring suit. Seligman hired an economist, Marc Bendick, to analyze the employment data that Wal-Mart, like all companies, provides yearly to the EEOC. Bendick, who has been an expert witness in more than 100 employment discrimination cases and has testified for both employees and employers, found that women made up over 60 percent of Wal-Mart's hourly workers, but just 33 percent of management. Comparable retailers such as Target had on average about the same proportion of women in the nonsalaried workforce, but on average nearly 50 percent of managers were women. Even more striking, when Bendick compared Wal-Mart stores to competitors in the same location, he found little geographic variation in these ratios, and little change over time. In fact, the percentage of women among Wal-Mart's management in 1999, 34.5 percent, was less than that of its competitors in 1975, 38.4 percent. According to Bendick, the statistical likelihood that this difference between Wal-Mart and its competitors could have arisen by chance and not intention—in other words, discrimination on Wal-Mart's part—was "very many times less than one chance in many billions."

Bendick's study showed that Wal-Mart was far more centralized than its competitors, and that an unusually large percentage of its managers was concentrated at headquarters—in 1999, 15.4 percent.[4] This is about twice the percentage of competitors' managers located at headquarters, 8.1 percent. Again, the 1999 figure was hardly a fluke: the percentage of management located at headquarters has been two to three times that of its competitors since 1975. That finding was significant because it suggested such a high degree of control by Bentonville over the company's operations, making it likely that the problem was systemic, and that the company, rather than a few individuals, was responsible for sex discrimination.

As soon as Seligman saw Bendick's data, he knew he wanted to be part of this case. "There are very few nationwide class actions because of the difficulty of showing common patterns throughout the country," he explains. "But this company seemed to be very centralized [and]. . . the statistical disparity [between percentages of women managers at Wal-Mart and other retailers] seemed to exist everywhere."

Tinkler and Seligman continued to build their coalition, knowing that taking on Wal-Mart would require a large team with varied expertise, as well as deep pockets. Seligman called Steve Stemmerman and Betty Lawrence, two San Francisco labor lawyers with the labor rights firm Davis, Cowell & Bowe who had extensive experience representing members of the United Food and Commercial Workers Union (UFCW) against Wal-Mart. They were delighted to join the legal team. In Seligman's first conversation with Stemmerman about this case, he says, "I mentioned the word 'Wal-Mart' to Steve and his response was, 'Evil empire.'"

This view is not uncommon among people fighting for the rights of retail workers. With its low wages and illegal union-busting tactics, Wal-Mart had drastically lowered industry standards. The UFCW, which represents retail workers, had been trying for years to organize Wal-Mart employees. Recently it had dramatically stepped up its efforts, as the anti-union retail giant moved into the grocery industry and competed ruthlessly with unionized supermarkets by under-cutting their prices and thus their business. The supermarkets were beginning to respond by rolling back their employees' benefits and wages so that they too could slash prices. By initiating this ugly dynamic Wal-Mart had incurred so much resentment that when union organizers heard about the sex discrimination suit, they were eager to join the fight. In fact, when the emerging coalition in June 2000 set up an 800 number to find plaintiffs and witnesses for the case, the union promptly made up a flyer advertising the case and the phone number, and distributed it in Wal-Mart parking lots nationwide.

The coalition Seligman put together consisted of three nonprofit organizations (the Impact Fund, Equal Rights Advocates, and the Public Justice Center, based in Baltimore) and three private firms (Cohen, Milstein, Hausfeld & Toll; Davis, Cowell & Bowe; and Tinkler & Bennett). The biggest of the for-profit law firms was Cohen, Milstein, Hausfeld & Toll, based in Washington, D.C., which would end up bearing the greatest financial burden. Well known for 28 years as a plaintiffs' class-action firm, it represents minority employees challenging discriminatory promotional practices at the highest corporate levels. Joe Sellers, the firm's leading attorney on the case and the plaintiffs' co-counsel, has a breadth of courtroom experience similar to Seligman's; he has litigated more than 25 civil-rights class actions.

Equal Rights Advocates (ERA) is a San Francisco-based nonprofit specializing in women's rights; as the only group in the coalition that works exclusively on women's issues, it brings an important feminist perspective to the suit. Partly because of its scant resources for media outreach and publicity, the ERA's lawyers, Sheila Thomas, Doris Ng, and Debra Smith, have received less press attention than Brad Seligman or Joseph Sellers. "It's ironic that this case is all about women and women's rights, but anything written about the lawyers has focused on the men," says Smith. The organization has provided personal representation to several of the plaintiffs, as well as much of the support for the lawsuit's hotline. The ERA office is cramped, and the attorneys must work in cubicles. *Dukes v. Wal-Mart* has been a considerable financial burden on ERA, requiring technological upgrades beyond its budget, and huge amounts of staff time, but the group is dedicated to pursuing the suit.

The Public Justice Center is a public-interest firm that uses litigation to bring about systemic reform in the legal system.

Despite its intimidating costs, the case against Wal-Mart is a public interest lawyer's dream. Wal-Mart's size and status as an industry leader mean that the suit could have a dramatic effect on the retail industry as a whole, a sector that employs 11 percent of America's working women. Stephanie Odle's case would prove to be a historic one.

"A Couple Knuckleheads"

Stephanie Odle and her emerging coalition of lawyers were not the first to observe, and decry, sex discrimination at Wal-Mart. The problem has a long history, and some of the most candid acknowledgments of the company's female troubles have come from unlikely sources. Sam Walton, writing in his 1992 autobiography *Made in America*, makes this point:

> Traditionally, we've had the attitude that if you wanted to be a manager at Wal-Mart, you basically had to be willing to move at a moment's notice. . . . Maybe that was necessary back in the old days, and maybe it was more rigid than it needed to be. Now, though, it's not really appropriate anymore. . . .[The requirement] really put good, smart women at a disadvantage in our company because at that time they weren't as free to pick up and move as many men were. Now I've seen the light on the opportunities we missed out on with women.

Walton then admits that his wife, Helen, and his daughter, Alice, helped him "come around to this way of thinking."[5] (In his book, Sam indulgently describes Helen as "a bit of a feminist,"[6] and several of her children have upheld her values by becoming major donors to Planned Parenthood.) In reality, employees say, the relocation policy never changed, and persists even today, though Wal-Mart officials have given conflicting answers on this point when deposed by plaintiffs' lawyers.

Asked about Sam Walton's reflections in August 2002, while still in the beginning phases of the discovery (evidence-gathering) process in the would-be class-action suit, Seligman laughed and said, "Sam Walton's going to be one of our witnesses!" Indeed, the plaintiffs are using this passage from Walton's book as evidence against Wal-Mart, because it shows that even at the very highest level of the company, the officials were aware that certain Wal-Mart policies were detrimental to women. This makes it particularly damning that these policies were never changed.

In fact, despite some impressive insights, Walton showed only minimal interest in the status of women at Wal-Mart. Even in 1985 the company's top 42 officers included no women, and the board of directors was similarly female-free. In his 2000 book, Bob Ortega identifies Walton's own lack of interest in the problem as a major culprit.[7]

Ortega recounts board members' attempts to get women and African Americans on the 15-member board. One of those pushing for more diversity was Jim Jones, a banker, who called Walton "really resistant to the idea." After balking for a while, Walton finally offered Betsy Sanders, then a Nordstrom vice president and general manager, a seat. But Nordstrom didn't want Sanders to serve on another retailer's board of directors, so she had to turn down the directorship.

Walton's wife and daughter had an even more celebrated candidate in mind. Her law firm represented Wal-Mart frequently, and she was a shareholder as well as the wife of the governor of Arkansas, where Wal-Mart is headquartered. Helen and Alice lobbied hard to convince Sam to appoint Hillary Rodham Clinton to the Wal-Mart board. Though the Clintons and the Waltons were friends, Sam was at best lukewarm to the idea.[8] Ortega speculates that the retail mogul may have disliked Clinton's liberalism: she had been actively crusading for a higher sales tax to fund the state's abysmal school system, and for high school health clinics to distribute condoms and other contraceptives.[9] In November 1986, the persistence of the Walton women paid off, and Hillary Clinton became Wal-Mart's first female board member, a position for which she accepted $15,000 a year.[10]

Just before Clinton arrived, Wal-Mart had hired an outside consultant to study the company's record on promoting women and people of color. "The track record, to no one's great surprise, was abysmal," Ortega writes. At the 1987 annual meeting, when asked why the company had so few female managers, Sam Walton said, "We haven't gotten as far as we would like. . . [but we have] a strong-willed young lady on the board now who has already told the board it should do more to ensure the advancement of women." At that time, 3 percent of Wal-Mart's store managers were women.

Clinton did make some headway at Wal-Mart: by 1989, there were two female vice presidents among Wal-Mart's top

88 officers, although the company's top 22 positions still did not include a single woman.[11] (Senator Clinton would not comment on her work with Wal-Mart, citing, through a spokeswoman, a policy of refusing interviews for book projects.) She resigned in 1992 to devote herself to her husband's presidential campaign. That year, at the shareholder meeting, when Bud Walton, Sam's brother and the company's cofounder, asked the crowd how the meeting could be improved, someone shouted, "Put some women on the board!" and a rowdy cheer filled the room.[12] The following year, Clinton's seat on the board was filled by Betsy Sanders, who had, by then, left Nordstrom.

That passion quickly dissipated. Even as the company modernized and expanded, becoming a leader in the use of technology and increasing its global presence by opening stores in Mexico and Hong Kong, its attitudes toward women remained archaic, reminiscent of the 1950s. Within the company, Wal-Mart's failure to promote women was discussed, but was never successfully addressed. In internal memos, top company executives lamented that Wal-Mart was "behind the rest of the world" in promoting women. In the early 1990s, a series of letters that was signed by more than 100 Wal-Mart and Sam's Clubs managers and was addressed to Helen Walton, Rob Walton (Sam Walton's son and the chair of the company's board of directors), and several top company executives, described a pattern of discrimination against women in promotions and of retaliation against women who complained. The letters, which were also sent to store managers nationwide, asked that the company's leaders take action. Little action was taken, though. In 1992, women at Wal-Mart's Bentonville headquarters formed a committee called the Women in Leadership Group. It undertook a study and completed a report in 1996 that found serious problems in the Wal-Mart culture, including widespread agreement that "stereotypes limit opportunities offered to women" at the company and a perception that "aggressive women intimidate men." After completing this report, the Women in Leadership Group disbanded, not to be heard from again until 2002, the year after the lawsuit was filed.

Meanwhile, every year throughout the 1990s, a group of nuns attended the company's shareholder meetings to call attention to sex and race discrimination. The nuns tried to prevail upon fellow shareholders to pass a resolution demanding public disclosure of race and sex statistics at the company, as well as regular reports on Wal-Mart's progress in removing barriers for women and racial minorities.

Sister Barbara Aires, of the Sisters of Charity of St. Elizabeth, based in Convent Station, New Jersey, was a leader in this effort. Given her order's history of work on behalf of women, this made sense. The Sisters of Charity was founded in 1809, and throughout much of the nineteenth century they championed the rights of working women. In 1899 the group founded the College of St. Elizabeth, New Jersey's first four-year college for women and one of the first colleges for women in the United States. Now, using their order's endowment to invest in a variety of large companies, including Wal-Mart, the Sisters continue the tradition. Working with the Interfaith Center on Corporate Responsibility, which since the 1970s has been one of the leading socially conscious shareholder pressure groups, the nuns have been demanding better public reporting of Wal-Mart's employment data and have also been among those pressing, with some success, for more female directors on the board.

At shareholder meetings, the nuns are an arresting moral presence in an environment in which, despite Wal-Mart's reputation as a Christian company, profit reigns supreme over all ethical systems. They also stand out because few of Wal-Mart's critics attend shareholder meetings. Many corporate meetings are besieged by activists urging that companies pay more attention to social justice. Wal-Mart attracts very few, in part because the meeting's location in Fayetteville, Arkansas, is remote and expensive for activists (many of whom live on the coasts) to get to. In 2003, a planned convergence of labor and women's groups, who were going to gather outside the meeting to protest Wal-Mart's abuses against workers, was canceled because so few people could make the trip. Many local activists avoid the meeting for another reason. Wanda Stephens, an activist with NOW and People for the American Way, who lives in Fayetteville, says the region is totally dominated by Wal-Mart, so much so that even progressives can't publicly object to its practices. "A lot of our people are involved with Wal-Mart," she says. "Some work there, some hold stock, and all of us shop there." If she and other NOW activists were to protest Wal-Mart's treatment of women, Stephens says, it would alienate too many people: "It would limit our effectiveness in other areas."

A few local activists were brave enough to protest the 2004 meeting. But, the continued powerful presence at annual meetings of the Sisters of Charity is crucial. Whereas mainstream feminist groups can't even get Wal-Mart officials to return their phone calls, the company is obligated to take the nuns seriously as a force of Christian righteousness, and has had frequent meetings with them. At the 2003 meeting, Rob Walton took pains to stress his long-running dialogue with Aires. "While we don't always agree with her," he said warmly, and a bit nervously, "we always respect her views." Aires returns the respect, stressing that Wal-Mart officials have been open to her perspective. "I don't find the current leadership of Wal-Mart arrogant at all. Even if they are particularly angry with me right now for shareholders' resolutions, if I called someone out there they would talk to me," she says, adding, "I do think they are upset that we are so persistent."

As Sister Aires has recently begun pointing out at shareholder meetings, the lawsuit seemed an inevitable outcome of a company's failure to listen to its critics, and to its female workers, who responded to the legal coalition's 800 number with great enthusiasm. Along with the UFCW, Stephanie Odle and her friends spread the word that they were looking for participants in a class-action suit. The legal team needed to find more women who were willing to come forward as plaintiffs. Although it was a national suit, with plaintiffs from all over the country, because it was filed in the Ninth Circuit federal court in San Francisco, the lawyers thought the lead plaintiff should be from California. The named plaintiffs also needed to have certain personal qualities. "In a class case," Brad Seligman explains, "you have a small number of women who stand for everybody. It requires somebody who not only has [her own] claim, but also has the intestinal fortitude and sense of the fiduciary duty of the job. They've got to put the class first, not their own interest. It's a special kind of person." In this particular case, he added, it's got to be "somebody who's willing to stand up against what is now the largest company in the world."

The plaintiffs found that person in Betty Dukes; in spring 2001 she became the lead plaintiff, and the suit became *Betty Dukes v. Wal-Mart Stores, Inc.* When I met Dukes, a confident woman who speaks in preacherly cadences, she was wearing a colorful headwrap and a flattering silky orange blouse. Impassioned and sure of herself, she fully appreciates the social implications of her grievance. She has what she frankly refers to as a "dark past": numerous misdemeanor convictions, mostly for fire-arms possession, and DUI, but that may not matter. "You hardly ever get the perfect plaintiff," says Betty Lawrence, one of Betty Dukes's attorneys and an associate with Davis, Cowell & Bowe. "Most people have skeletons in their closet." (In one of Lawrence's other employment class-action suits, for example, the lead plaintiff had done time for armed robbery. "But otherwise, he's a great plaintiff," says Lawrence, with dark amusement. "He's really articulate, and understands the issues.")

A leader in her community and in her church, Betty Dukes is deeply offended that Wal-Mart doesn't afford her the respect she deserves. Because of her prominence in Pittsburg, California, she views Wal-Mart's treatment of her as an insult not only to her but also to the town, which she has considered home since 1960, the year she and her family moved there from Louisiana. "Wal-Mart, coming to Pittsburg, is coming into my world," says Dukes. "My family is just as important in Pittsburg as Wal-Mart is." Wal-Mart has only been in Pittsburg since 1991—a newcomer compared to the Dukes family. Betty Dukes feels that her demotion hurt her own and her family's standing in the town, humiliating her not only at work but also before a broader public.

Pittsburg, California (population 47,564), is not a typical Wal-Mart town in that it's only half an hour from San Francisco, and is on the Bay Area Rapid Transit (BART) system. But it is typical of the places Wal-Mart sets up mega-shop in that it's seen more prosperous days. Known in the nineteenth century as the New York of the Pacific—actually named New York Landing for a time—Pittsburg, located on the Sacramento River, was a hub for the fishing and canning industries. In 1911, when Columbia Geneva Steel opened a plant, New York Landing's citizens voted to name their town Pittsburg after the Pennsylvania steel capital, but lopped off the final *h* to make it easier to spell. Pittsburg's steel industry thrived for decades and reached its peak in the 1950s. Then a slide downward started, and by November 2003, Pittsburg had an unemployment rate of 7.1 percent, significantly higher than either the national or state average that month. Towns like Pittsburg tend to welcome Wal-Mart, as their struggling citizens love its low prices. Besides, these towns lack industries that might provide better jobs, and particularly given the near collapse of the U.S. welfare system in the mid-1990s, Wal-Mart's low-wage jobs were better than none.

Nevertheless, Dukes still feels it's important that her roots are deeper than Wal-Mart's. Referring to a common Wal-Mart business practice, Betty Dukes says, "Wal-Mart may close up and say, 'We're not making money in the Pittsburg store. We're gonna close up Pittsburg and move on.' But Betty Dukes can't close up Pittsburg and move on."

Although *Dukes v. Wal-Mart* is about sex discrimination, not race discrimination, two of the plaintiffs have also filed claims of racial discrimination against the company. Betty Dukes is one of them. According to Dukes, the supervisor who demoted her referred to himself as a "redneck." She acknowledges that the word is used lightly in Wal-Mart (and also the wider) culture, perhaps sometimes harmlessly. "We sell 'redneck' greeting cards," she says, laughing as she alludes to a line of "redneck" American Greetings cards, sold exclusively at Wal-Mart, that features jokes by the comedian Jeff Foxworthy. But when Dukes's supervisor said he was "'proud to be a redneck,' I didn't take it as a greeting card. No, I did not. I took it more intense than that." Some of her fellow workers—blacks and Hispanics—"felt a little intimidated by him just using the expression. They felt that maybe he could see himself a little bit superior to them." Some Hispanic coworkers approached Dukes, a bit hesitantly, asking her to explain the term. "They weren't exactly sure what 'redneck' meant," she recalls, "but they didn't like it." Language like that contributed to Dukes's conviction that her demotion was racially motivated.

Thearsa Collier is another *Dukes v. Wal-Mart* witness who experienced race as well as sex discrimination on the job, sometimes simultaneously. Collier says her Geneva, Alabama, store manager told her, sarcastically, that as "a black" and a woman she would go far with Wal-Mart. In a statement for the plaintiffs made in support of the motion for class certification, she testified, "I knew from his tone of voice he would never give me a fair chance to succeed." Like Dukes, she also found the man's use of the word "redneck" intimidating: "We're all rednecks here, so you might as well get used to it," he said. (A subsequent investigation by Wal-Mart confirmed that Collier's store manager had made the statement.)

Still, although there's plenty of anecdotal evidence of racism at Wal-Mart, and a few individuals have brought—and won—lawsuits charging race discrimination, the company is plagued less by systemic racism than by systemic sexism. In contrast to the percentage of women in management—which are consistently low nationwide—those of racial minorities vary dramatically depending on a store's location. At Wal-Mart, members of minority groups are promoted to management positions at far better rates than women—that is, in percentages closer to their representation in Wal-Mart workforce and in local labor markets.

Wal-Mart has also responded more promptly to charges of racism, and has taken the concerns of racial minorities more seriously than those of women. In early 1999 Jesse

Jackson sent a letter to Wal-Mart in which he expressed concern about race discrimination at the company and asked to have a meeting. Wal-Mart officials went crazy and sent off a flurry of internal memos in which they enumerated everything they were doing to fight racism at the company. Jackson never followed up, but a short letter from him was enough to provoke distress at Wal-Mart's highest levels. Coleman Peterson, vice president until early 2004 of Wal-Mart's People Division, Wal-Mart's populist-sounding name for its human resources division, is black and serves on the board of the NAACP. "Wal-Mart may well have paid more attention to race issues [than women's issues], coming out of the seventies in a border South state," Seligman hypothesizes.

From 2001 to mid-2003, lawyers on both sides of *Dukes v. Wal-Mart* gathered evidence to bolster their arguments for and against class certification. The plaintiffs were preparing to argue that they should be allowed to represent the largest group of women ever to bring such a case, whereas Wal-Mart prepared to argue that these women represented themselves and no one else. Mona Williams, Wal-Mart's spokeswoman, quoted in *Fortune* magazine, did not question the individual plaintiffs' stories, but said such abuses did not show that the company had a systemic sex discrimination problem. The trouble, she remarked memorably, was "a couple knuckleheads out there who do dumb things"—sexist bad apples who create isolated incidents.[13]

More women joined the lawsuit as named plaintiffs: Kimberly Miller of Ocala, Florida; Patricia Sturgeson of Vacaville,

California; Micki Miller Earwood of Springfield, Ohio; and Sandra Stevenson of Gurnee, Illinois. On December 3, 2001, however, Judge Martin Jenkins ruled that the named plaintiffs had to be from California, though he allowed nationwide discovery—gathering evidence from all over the country—and the possibility of a nationwide class.

Of that group, only Dukes and Sturgeson could remain as named plaintiffs, as both were from California. Stephanie Odle, who now lives in Norman, Oklahoma, says, "It's kind of strange because I started this whole thing, and then I had to step aside."

On September 10, 2002, Judge Jenkins extended the scope of the discovery process by significantly expanding the time period for which both evidence could be gathered and from which the class of potential plaintiffs and witnesses could be recruited, from December 26, 1999, to December 26, 1998. Now, the class could include any woman employed by Wal-Mart since that date, and the plaintiffs were allowed to include some important evidence from that period, particularly some internal documents from 1998 and 1999 in which company officials express concern about the lack of women in management positions. Wal-Mart's attorneys recognized the significance of the move and promptly attempted to appeal the decision, but Judge Jenkins ruled against them. In the same ruling, he allowed the plaintiffs to add five more named plaintiffs—or class representatives— to the case.

One of these was Christine Kwapnoski, who had been employed in a Concord, California, Sam's Club, for the company for 15 years (she still works there). A small, light-haired tomboy, Kwapnoski jokes that Sarah Michelle Gellar could play her in a movie about this lawsuit. "'The Wal-Mart Slayer,'" she says with a laugh. "It could either be a sitcom or a tragedy." She is currently the only salaried manager named as a plaintiff, which is crucial, because testimony from salaried managers appeals more broadly to middle-class public sympathies, because—however unfairly—managers may be perceived as being more competent and hard-working than their wage-earning colleagues. The public also sees them as having more to lose by turning against the company.

Kwapnoski began working for Sam's Club in Grandview, Missouri, in 1987, when she was 22. Seven years later, she was selected to help open a new Sam's Club in Concord. Once there, her supervisors, delighted by her talents and work ethic, encouraged her to transfer permanently, which she did in 1994. Kwapnoski has been named "associate of the month" more times than she can remember. For years she asked to join the management training program, but her request was denied. In the beginning she used to write this request on all her evaluations in the space for "associate's comments." But, she says, "I eventually stopped writing it down, because it was never happening." She was repeatedly turned down when she applied for promotions; meanwhile, men with less experience and less tenure with the company were promoted over her. One man, who had been demoted from a supervisory position he "couldn't handle," was promoted over her three times. She was consistently paid less than her male colleagues.

Kwapnoski says she was reluctant at first to join *Dukes v. Wal-Mart,* fearing that Wal-Mart would retaliate against her. Ultimately, though, she has realized that she is an exceptional employee. "I'm not afraid of Wal-Mart. That's what keeps a lot of women from [publicly joining the lawsuit]. They are really afraid for their jobs." Kwapnoski embodies the confidence a worker must have to stand up to Wal-Mart. "I can always get another job. I have enough talents. I think I could be a manager at Home Depot."

She filed her complaint with the EEOC in February 2002, and joined *Dukes v. Wal-Mart* later that year. Since then she has been promoted, and is now an assistant manager in the bakery department. Kwapnoski's ex-husband's wife works for Wal-Mart and is hostile to Kwapnoski's involvement in the lawsuit; she has asked Kwapnowski's kids whether their mother is "in it for the money." Kwapnoski laughs. "She says she's never had any problems in her Wal-Mart. Well, good for you. I'll be one of the people who makes sure you don't have any problems in the future!"

Cleo Page, who joined the suit after Judge Jenkins's 2002 ruling broadening the scope of possible plaintiffs, had led a sheltered life in a devoutly Christian family. She began working for Wal-Mart when she needed a job quickly because "my mother needed a birthday gift!"

Hired to work in the returns department in the Livermore, California, store in the fall of 1998, Page was promoted to a customer-service manager position within a couple of months. She had already worked as a cashier in

Tulsa, Oklahoma, and then had relocated to California to work in Union City. Her coworkers in Livermore voted her "best customer- service manager" in the store. It looked as if she had a future with Wal-Mart. But her hopes were dampened when she interviewed a little over a year later for another promotion, this time to head the men's clothing department. She was told by an assistant manager that it was a "man's world," and that men controlled management positions at Wal-Mart. She was offered that job, but management later reconsidered and gave the position to a white woman. (Page, who is black, also has a race discrimination claim against Wal-Mart that, like Dukes's race-related charges, are not part of the class-action suit.)

Page complained about her treatment, and told the store manager that she wanted a career at Wal-Mart, that she hoped eventually to obtain a salaried management position. In 1999 she applied for a job as a support manager, the highest-ranking wage-paying position at Wal-Mart and the largest feeder for salaried management. She wasn't hired, and a less-qualified white male got the job instead. She was eventually promoted to department manager, first in men's clothing, then in boy's clothing. But her progress stopped there. In 2000 she applied for two more support-manager positions but was rejected. The store manager told her it was because she needed training and experience working in a larger department, but never helped her to get that training or experience.

Page often heard male department managers and assistant managers complain that "women were taking over" the store and ask each other if they knew other men who would be interested in working at Wal-Mart. In November 2000 Page was unfairly disciplined and realized with frustration that she was never going to be promoted. She quit.

When Page left Wal-Mart, she and her mother, who had moved to California together from Tulsa, lost the house they'd been trying to buy. As a consequence of their sudden homelessness, the state took away two foster children the women had been trying to adopt. Devastated, Cleo and her mother moved back to Tulsa, where the rest of their family lives. (For the purposes of the lawsuit she is still a California plaintiff, because the discrimination she is charging took place in California.)

In April 1996, after 30 years of retail experience, Deborah ("Dee") Gunter, then 46 and the mother of five grown children, began working at a Riverside, California, Wal-Mart as a cashier in the photo lab, making $5.50 an hour. Loudly confident with, in her words, "a huge ego," Gunter was sure she'd advance in the company. "I'm one of those people who can work at a job for two months and learn to run the whole show," she says. "I thought I'd go beyond store manager. I intended to be up in corporate."

But first she hoped to head the pet department. It seemed an obvious position for a passionate animal lover with three decades of experience breeding and raising show dogs (she now raises and shows llamas as well). Gunter, whose résumé also included a stint as a vet's assistant, was rejected three times for the pet department job because, she was told, she didn't have enough experience. The job went twice to teenage boys. Still nonplussed, she exclaims, "I've also had rabbits, lizards, guinea pigs, snakes, cats, goats, horses, along with the dogs and the llamas, but I didn't know anything!"

She applied for management positions and was repeatedly passed over as less experienced men were promoted. When she was transferred to the Tire and Lube Express (TLE) department, in Perris, California, about 20 miles from Riverside, she did the work of a support manager without the title or the pay. She was never trained for the job either, despite her many requests for training. It was the same Catch-22 as Page's: the manager of the TLE told her she could not be a support manager because she lacked the training, yet her requests for training were continually denied. Though she did eventually get a small raise, she never got the promotion.

She trained two men as support managers in the TLE department, and both of them were promoted into the position. Her supervisor sexually harassed her, suggesting, after she'd had a fight with her husband, "Why don't you put your face in my lap and take care of both of our problems?" When she complained, her hours were reduced, she says, and nothing was done about the harassment. Hoping to get more hours, she transferred to the nearby Lake Elsinore store, where she was hired as a cashier and clerk in the TLE. Once again, she trained a man to fill the support-manager job; once again, he was promoted and got the title and salary— and her hours were reduced. She complained about her reduced hours and requested a meeting with the district manager to protest this discriminatory treatment. On the day her meeting was scheduled, in mid-August 1999, the store manager fired her.

A conservative Republican and fundamentalist Christian, Gunter insists that she's "no women's libber. But this isn't the Stone Ages, and this isn't the age of Scarlett O'Hara." She joined the *Dukes* case as a plaintiff after seeing a report about the case on the morning news. She was livid to see that other women at Wal-Mart were suffering the same indignities, and wanted to do whatever she could do to help. She called the *Dukes* legal team and offered to be a witness, but her case was so convincing that she became a plaintiff.

Gunter's husband, a retired Teamster, is angry at the way Wal-Mart treated Dee. He still wants to drive down to the Perris store and beat up the fellow who made lewd comments to his wife. Gunter smilingly shakes her head at him, reminding him of the lawsuit. "I tell him, 'This way is better,'" she says. "'This is the Christian way.'"

Edith Arana also lives in the Los Angeles area. She was hired as the personnel manager before a new store in Duarte, a working-class suburb of Los Angeles, had even opened, and began working there in September 1995. With more than ten years of retail experience, she was surprised that such a large company would pay her so poorly—$7 an hour—but she wholeheartedly committed herself to Wal-Mart because managers assured her that she'd have many opportunities to advance in the company. Then 35 and a married mother of five, she worked such long hours at the store that her family had a grim joke about her dedication: "Forward her mail to Wal-Mart!"

After almost two years, Arana was promoted to the hourly position of support manager. She repeatedly told her store manager, John Kocharian, that she wanted to go into the assistant-manager training program. Kocharian blew her off with vague, noncommittal answers, sometimes simply a dismissive shrug. At one point he all but admitted that he didn't want any women in the training program, saying, "There's no room for people like you."

Though his words sound ambiguous, in the context the meaning was clear to Arana: it was another example of Kocharian's dismissive treatment of women. She then realized that, in fact, women at the Duarte Wal-Mart were rarely promoted to management positions. She used the Wal-Mart 800 number—widely heralded by the company as a sign of its "Open Door Policy" toward employees but known by many workers as "1-800-YOU'RE FIRED"—to complain about Kocharian's treatment of women.

In response to her complaints, Arana charges, she was transferred to a less desirable position, that of "inventory traveler," meaning she had to drive throughout the region taking inventory in far-away stores, often leaving her young children for as long as a week at a time. During her tenure at Wal-Mart, Arana had to take several leaves of absence for stress, on her doctor's orders.

She kept complaining. Eventually, in October 2001, after her hours had been cut significantly and she had been disciplined for absurd reasons (like helping a customer instead of taking her lunch break), she was accused of "stealing time"— a charge frequently fabricated by retail managers who want to get rid of troublemakers—and was fired. She denies the accusation and asserts that she was fired in retaliation for complaining about discrimination. Arana, an African American, is not charging the company with race discrimination. "I was not promoted because I am a woman," she says, "and I am *positive* of that."

Arana knows she was a superb employee. "I am more than good at what I do," she says. She is profoundly disappointed that Wal-Mart failed to recognize her own gifts, but is just as upset about the company's failure to reward the hard work and dedication of her female coworkers. She thinks of all the times they didn't get the raises and promotions they deserved, while those rewards went to men. "I'm not just doing this for me," she says. "I'm doing it for all the women in my store that have done their best. I can still see their faces. I see their anguish and disappointment."

Many women are eager to go back to Wal-Mart if the *Dukes* plaintiffs win the lawsuit, but Arana, now 43 and training to become a preschool teacher, has moved on. "In a fantasy world I'd go back because everything would be okay, but this is not fantasy. This is true life." She explains that in order to look realistically at Wal-Mart, the company she believed in so fervently, she had "to grow up a lot." Having outgrown her trust in the company, a trust she now considers naïve and childish, Arana doubts she could go back now. The company has behaved in a way that is profoundly at odds with her own values, and she wants nothing to do with it. "I just don't believe that I [wouldn't] be tainted."

The class certification hearing was held September 24, 2003, before Judge Jenkins and a packed courtroom. The plaintiffs asked the judge to certify a class of 1.6 million women. The size of the class was unprecedented, but plaintiffs' attorneys argued that the discrimination was consistent across regions and Wal-Mart was sufficiently centralized in its operations to warrant such a historic legal move. Wal-Mart argued that the class was unmanageably large and would result in an impossibly complicated trial, as they attempted to show. The plaintiffs, Wal-Mart said, would have to establish a disparity between men and women's pay within each of Wal-Mart's nearly 4,000 stores. One trial day would have to be devoted to each store, resulting in a 13-year trial.

Judge Jenkins listened carefully to the arguments on both sides, and the hearing lasted the entire day. Whatever he decided, his decision would be closely scrutinized, as the losing side was almost certain to appeal. He would not announce his ruling until June 2004. Despite the case's magnitude, it was legally straightforward; its true significance was political and cultural. At stake was Wal-Mart's prominent place in American culture—where the company is well loved—despite criticisms and its status as a role model for other businesses. At stake, too, was Wal-Mart's image among its own employees, upon whose sometimes mystifying dedication the company's phenomenal success depends.

2

"MADE IN AMERICA": THE WAL-MART CULTURE AND ITS PROMISES

"WHOSE WAL-MART IS IT?" the Wal-Mart executive bellowed. 20,000 enthusiasts—most of them Wal-Mart employees—roared back, "It's my Wal-Mart!" It was Wal-Mart's 2003 annual meeting, held in early June at the Bud Walton Arena, one of many buildings on the University of Arkansas's Fayetteville campus named after members of the Walton family (Sam Walton's brother, Bud, was an integral part of the company's early success.). Evoking by turns a revival meeting and a riotous football game, this call-and-response ritual was repeated throughout the day with passionate enthusiasm, often as part of a much stranger series of antics known as "the Wal-Mart cheer."

The cheer filled the arena, and it is an amazing spectacle. "Give me a 'W'! Give me an 'A'! Give me an 'L'! Give me a 'Squiggley!'" Thousands waggled their hips for the "Squiggley" in an inventive bodily enactment of the star in the middle of the company's name. "Give me an 'M'! Give me an 'A'! Give me an 'R'! Give me a 'T'! Whose Wal-Mart is it?"

"My Wal-Mart!" they yelled with gusto. The cheer was introduced by Sam Walton, who was inspired by witnessing a similar display of team spirit in a South Korean factory in 1975.

One of the most celebrated (and reviled, especially by some workers and observers who find it "cultlike") of Wal-Mart's quirks is the company culture, which is rich with shared language, values, and rituals. The annual meeting offers one of the most striking windows into Wal-Mart. In fact, almost nothing of substance gets decided there. Apart from voting on a few, mostly symbolic, resolutions, the event has no purpose but to immerse Wal-Mart workers, shareholders, and analysts in company culture and to show that Wal-Mart is a great place to work.

Employees from South Korea, Brazil, Argentina, and Japan who attended the meeting did the Wal-Mart cheer in their native tongues. "Guess it works in any language," one executive declared proudly from the podium. But these efforts at internationalism sometimes seemed forced. When a stadium-wide cheer in Spanish faltered, or when an American speaker said "North Korea" when he meant South Korea, people laughed, recognizing that the gaffe reflected the gathering's American—and provincial—character. Presentations from "Wal-Mart USA" drew boisterous foot stomping, whistling cheers, and a flag-waving standing ovation, whereas presentations from international divisions received only polite applause. Throughout the meeting, American flags adorned either side of the podium, and more than one performer led the crowd in a rousing rendition of the "Star-Spangled Banner." The message was clear: Wal-Mart is America—and vice versa.

This premise is surprisingly widely accepted. In 1992, the first President Bush awarded Sam Walton the nation's highest honor, the Presidential Medal of Freedom, saying, "This is not about Sam's wealth. He's earned it and that's his business. . . . His vision is about what's fundamentally good and right about this country."

Sam Walton and his successors have been geniuses at myth production. Because of a brief, much-touted initiative in 1985 to sell some products made in the United States, many Americans still believe that Wal-Mart goods are made by American workers. In fact at least 85 percent of Wal-Mart products are made overseas, most of those in China, under sweatshop conditions, by workers, mostly women, who lack the right to organize. At the 2003 annual shareholder meeting, a man from Greenwood, Missouri, asked what percentage of Wal-Mart's goods were made in the United States. Tom Coughlin, Wal-Mart's CEO, didn't answer the question, but said, "We do everything we can, but first and foremost our responsibility is to bring value to customers." (Some Wal-Mart products are made in American Samoa, a U.S. territory with minimal legal protections for workers—technically American but not what the well-meaning customer has in mind when she sees the "Made in the USA" label.) But the "Made in America" slogan and its purely rhetorical value offers a metaphor for Wal-Mart's very American promises of mobility and reward, as well as respect for individual rights, God, and family.

Wal-Mart's professed values are, for many workers, the most compelling aspect of the Wal-Mart culture, because they are the professed values of the United States itself. Wal-Mart rhetoric is adamantly populist. Many speakers at the 2003 annual meeting explained the slogan "It's My Wal-Mart" by emphasizing that it is not "just a slogan." "From the very beginning, Wal-Mart has belonged to all of us," said one executive. Other Wal-Mart slogans, such as "Our People Make the Difference" convey similar messages, evoking respect for the worker. "Respect the Individual" is one of the "Three Basic Beliefs," established by Sam Walton and still part of every Wal-Mart worker's vocabulary.

When asked the secret of his own success, Sam Walton often credited the Wal-Mart workers, and his successor as CEO, David Glass, did the same. Glass is fond of referring to Wal-Mart as a company of "pretty ordinary people doing extraordinary things." Wal-Mart uses the term "associate," never "employee"; Sam's Club uses "partner." Such language seems flattering to many working people.

Wal-Mart literature makes much of founder Sam Walton's legacy. But it's not just a paper legacy: Wal-Mart workers speak often of their attachment to Walton's story and to his values. Even plaintiffs in *Dukes v. Wal-Mart* say they have a profound respect for Sam Walton. Dee Gunter, one of the *Dukes* plaintiffs, was inspired to work for Wal-Mart after meeting Walton at a public talk he gave in her town, in which he talked up his company. He "really, really cared about his people," she says.

Indeed, Wal-Mart culture constantly emphasizes a commitment to the common man. A down-home, plain-speaking manner is adopted at the highest levels. Sam Walton drove a pickup truck all his life, flew coach class, and despised executives who flaunted their wealth. To this day, the company's Bentonville headquarters is downright shabby-looking, and many high-level officials have basement offices. Even executives must share hotel rooms when they travel, and bring their own pencils to meetings. Of course, some of these practices have more to do with Wal-Mart's obsessive focus on the bottom line than with an actual affinity with Everyman, but the just-folks culture makes such peculiarities seem natural. At the 2003 annual meeting, the Christian pop icon Amy Grant, a multi-million-dollar-earning singer-songwriter, performed a number called "I Dream of Simple Things." Addressing the crowd before her performance, Grant said, "Simple things are what Wal-Mart is all about."

Wal-Mart likes to assure small-town rural Americans that it understands them in a way that other companies do not. At the 2003 annual meeting, CEO Coughlin said to great applause, "City people don't get Wal-Mart. Wal-Mart is for country people." (In reality, rural America's population is shrinking, and Wal-Mart has for the past decade been aggressively trying to expand into metro and suburban areas.) Many Wal-Mart workers proudly describe themselves as "country" and strongly identify with the company for this reason. The company also markets its image, hence its cheerful embrace of Jeff Foxworthy's "redneck" jokes and products. As company officials often say, Wal-Mart proved that a big discounter could prosper in rural America. While other retailers neglected country people, Wal-Mart always believed in them.

The story of Sam Walton and Wal-Mart is presented to employees, the media, and the public as a Horatio Alger tale, a rise from humble beginnings, and this triumph is the main plot line of Sam Walton's 1992 autobiography, *Made in America*. As a young man during the Depression, Walton put himself through the University of Missouri by turning his paper route into a profitable business with several employees. He also waited tables and worked as a lifeguard. He'd hoped to go to the Wharton School of Business at the University of Pennsylvania, but eventually realized that even as hard as he was working, he'd never be able to afford it. He became a salesman for J. C. Penney, where, he recalled, "I would screw up the sales slips and generally mishandle the cash register side of things." One supervisor told him, "Maybe you're just not cut out for retail."[1] Eventually he met and married Helen Robson, whose father was a successful and wealthy Oklahoma lawyer, banker, and rancher. Walton was able to borrow money from his father-in-law to start a retail business of his own. Walton was, of course, a genuine success, but as in most trailer-park-to-gazillionaire legends, privilege (in this case, Helen's) and luck played an indispensable role in his real story.

The Wal-Mart Visitors' Center, on the Bentonville town square on the site of the first Wal-Mart, features the original shabby storefront. Inside is displayed the founder's tiny original office completely intact, with a scribbled note on his desk: "Call Helen. At home." At every turn, the Visitors' Center presents Wal-Mart as the underdog who "proved the doubters wrong." Walton himself is always shown in plain work clothes and a shabby cap—rarely in a suit—and is constantly referred to as a man who "never turned his back on his roots."

In his book, Walton, the richest man in America, reflects on future generations of his family and expresses the hope that his values of thrift and hard work will be passed along. While admitting that "it's unrealistic of me to expect them all to get up and throw paper routes," he says, "I'd hate to see any descendants of mine fall into the category of what I'd call 'idle rich'—a group I've never had much use for."[2]

Even today, when (per *Forbes* magazine) five of the ten richest individuals in the world are members of the Walton family, it is possible for Brenda Barrerra, a call-center worker at company headquarters, to insist that "the Waltons are just normal people." Much of the general public believes this, too: a Bentonville-area cab driver who claimed—probably misleadingly—to have dated Alice Walton said that "she's just like you and me. Very down-to-earth."

Central to Wal-Mart's commitment to ordinary folk is a promise of advancement. The company constantly assures workers that Wal-Mart is a place of great opportunity and mobility, where hard work and sacrifice will be rewarded. Seventy percent of Wal-Mart managers come from its non-managerial workforce—those working for hourly wages—a fact mentioned often in Wal-Mart employee meetings, and a college degree is considered unimportant. Dee Gunter says, "They offered me the opportunity to go as high as I want without a college education. So I was thrilled to death to work for 'em."

Cleo Page, a plaintiff who worked at stores in Oklahoma and California, remembers that district managers would "tell you in the meetings that 'I started out as a push cart person'. . . and I'm thinking 'wow, if they did it then I can too.'" Each store has a picture of its store manager on the wall, and Page imagined hers would be hanging up there one day. Edith Arana, another plaintiff, agrees: "The impression I got was, as long as you work hard, there's nothing you can't do in this company."

Dukes v. Wal-Mart is, in fact, a product of this company culture. The plaintiffs believed fervently in Wal-Mart's promises, and the lawsuit originates in their disappointment. As American history shows, very often people who have taken the system at its word have ended up changing it. Vivian Gornick, a feminist writer who is working on a biography of Elizabeth Cady Stanton, an early advocate of woman suffrage, describes how Americans become activists: "Every American grows up imbued with this notion of the democracy and then if you're the wrong sex or the wrong class or the wrong color, you suddenly realize that *you* are not what they had in mind when they promised democracy. What happens then is this sense of outrage, of democracy denied. And that's totally American." When Stanton realized that she was a second-class citizen in this great democracy, Gornick says, "It burned in her forever. For fifty years without a stop."

In the same way, when people realize they aren't included in the Wal-Mart promise, their disillusionment is powerful. The *Dukes* plaintiffs and many of the witnesses are people who believed intensely in the Wal-Mart culture, hoped to advance in the company, and found out it didn't work for women. To Betty Dukes, Wal-Mart's rhetoric of opportunity rankles. "If you portray yourself to be a great place to work, a great place to grow and strive," she says, "then that's what you ought to be. . . . They have not lived up to their great reputation." Edith Arana says women in her store believed the company's promise that "if you do good, you get good." But if you're female, "You do good, you get nothing."

Arana encouraged other women's faith in the Wal-Mart culture. "You have ladies coming in here, they've had a lot going on in their life, and the company tells them: 'It doesn't matter, you're gonna succeed. Sometimes you'll make sacrifices, and we'll do for you,'" she recalls. "We would encourage each other." When her coworkers would complain about being asked to work beyond their obligation, Arana would tell them, "Just do it with a smile," assuring them that someday they'd be rewarded with a promotion. "I'd say,. . . 'Don't worry about it. Just go on and do it. Because these are sacrifices that pay off in the end.'"

Even as she was having her own doubts about Wal-Mart's promises, Arana tried to be upbeat when talking with her coworkers. "I'd try to come up with something to keep them still positive, because I'm thinking 'maybe it's just me, maybe I don't feel good today. *Maybe I just don't feel good today.*'" Arana is a charismatic woman with an air of motherly wisdom beyond her years, and her coworkers listened to her. But when she realized her own promotion, so often promised, was never going to come, she felt guilty about having encouraged so many other women to believe in the company. "What do you say now to these women who say, 'You told me to work hard, and I'd get this department'?"

Being a plaintiff in this lawsuit is Arana's way of making it up to her coworkers; she feels that she deceived them by being such a company booster. "Somebody has to stand up. . . . I'll take that responsibility. Everyday I keep picturing these women. . . . They may not have the strength or the will to [stand up to the company], but right now I do."

She also feels embarrassed about having believed the Wal-Mart promises. "I'm telling you," Arana says now, "I felt extremely used. I felt ashamed because I would have to tell somebody, 'I just went along with it.' I can just see people being like, 'Oh, duh!'" She continues, "If I can stop one person from feeling a percentage of the humiliation that I felt, then I will feel good about that. Because of all the times that I didn't say something." She compares Wal-Mart to a bad boyfriend: despite all the disappointing things he does, "you keep remembering when you first met him," and you keep on giving him another chance. "And that's how we get caught up," she continues. "They tell you exactly what you want to hear. But then you fall out of love and feel you were basically played."

Wal-Mart is widely seen as a company exemplifying "traditional values." Christian organizations ("Christian" as used here means fundamentalist and Evangelical) have had a great deal of success pressuring Wal-Mart not to sell music or magazines that offend their sensibilities, and these successes have helped to preserve the loyalty of the rural Christian, "family-values" segments of the population (despite recent secular-minded decisions, such as banning discrimination against gay workers). In fact, four out of the current six plaintiffs are, like many Wal-Mart customers, Evangelical Christians. They came to work for Wal-Mart believing that it was a Christian company. When Arana, a devout Christian and a devoted mother, first came to work at Wal-Mart, she was attracted to the company's "wholesomeness. I was interested in [Wal-Mart] because it seemed to be a family-oriented company."

To outsiders, sexism may seem almost predictable in a company so laden with the rhetoric of "traditional values," but the *Dukes* plaintiffs don't see it that way, and are acutely disillusioned, more so than if they'd been ill treated by a "non-Christian" company. To them, "Christian" values in no way justify Wal-Mart's unfair practices. Dukes believes that Wal-Mart's discrimination against women is profoundly "unspiritual." To her, "family values" include workplace fairness for women. "Not many women are home now like June Cleaver and Donna Reed," she says. "They're out there in the trenches trying to make a living for their families." Gunter, who like Dukes sings in her church choir, acknowledges some contradiction in her own beliefs. "As a Christian woman with a strong belief in my Bible, I don't believe a woman should be running the government or be a minister," she says. "But if she's qualified in the workplace she should be able to run it. So I'm kind of an oxymoron."

Employees constantly mention that Sam Walton was a family man and a devout Christian, although in real life he was neither—he did not have strong religious beliefs and rarely went to church, and Helen Walton often complained that he spent little time with his family. Yet even the *Dukes* plaintiffs are deeply invested in the myth of Walton as a religious man. "I believe Mr. Walton had a religious background," says Dukes, who proudly describes herself as "a preacher of the Gospel." Gunter believed Walton gave 10 percent of his income to his church, which also isn't true (Helen gave about $6 million to the Presbyterian Church U.S.A. and served on its board).

Wal-Mart makes frequent use of the phrase "Wal-Mart family," and Wal-Mart employees, asked what they like about the company, frequently cite the "family" feeling in the culture. Page says, "I liked the fact that, supposedly, we were family. All of us workers were always good friends, supportive when the kids were sick, or someone died. We took up a collection if they had to travel." Arana describes it as "kind of like a down-home, personal type of company. Like going to a girls' club for the day, except you're at work."

Employees' use of the word "family" reflects the ambiguous way Wal-Mart uses the word to imply both a close allegiance and loyalty between the employee and the company ("the Wal-Mart family") and to suggest Wal-Mart's consideration for actual families. The company's origins as a family-owned business are constantly emphasized. (To some extent, massive as it is, Wal-Mart is still a family firm; two of the 14-member board's directors are Waltons and Waltons own 1.68 billion shares, or 38 percent.) At the 2003 annual meeting, 83-year-old Helen Walton, Sam's now frail and infirm widow, drew roaring applause just by being wheeled into the room, though she said nothing.

"If you say you're family oriented, you have to be about family," says Dukes. Yet the notion that Wal-Mart is family-oriented is simply wishful thinking, since the company neither provides child care nor pays most workers enough to comfortably support families, or even, as Edith Arana points out, "enough to hire a baby-sitter."

Furthermore, many plaintiffs and witnesses in the lawsuit have had to make extraordinary family sacrifices for the company. Even though Arana was never promoted to a salaried position, she was constantly forced to put Wal-Mart's demands ahead of those of her family. Although she was a widow with young children, she would be sent on business trips to open new Wal-Mart stores for as long as a week at a time. When she objected and cited her family responsibilities, her manager would appeal to her dedication, saying, "Well, we all have family. We're all part of the Wal-Mart family."

For Arana, a woman passionately dedicated to her children and the memory of her late husband, this was the broken promise that hurt the most. She believed Wal-Mart's promise to be "family-friendly," a company that cared about family, and therefore the sacrifices she made toward her own family to keep her job would be rewarded. When she was never promoted, she was devastated by guilt over all the times she left her young children while she did Wal-Mart's bidding, and perhaps worse, regret for the times she had to leave her husband to go on the road (he died while she was working for Wal-Mart). She is still close to tears at the recollection: "It was very disheartening, very depressing. Because I would go back and think about all those times that I left my children, or my husband was sick and I left him. When I started thinking about all those sacrifices, I just got more and more depressed."

Really, just how Christian is Wal-Mart? Dukes, in addition to the sex discrimination she's faced, has discovered that Wal-Mart isn't a great place to work if you actually want to *practice* the Christian faith. For one thing, it's nearly impossible for a worker to be considered even for entry-level management if she can't work on Sundays. "I would think that they would want workers to have a religious background," she muses. "If you're pastoring a church and leading the flock of God, is Wal-Mart greater than God?" Dukes is also disturbed by some of the company's recent religious reversals—Wal-Mart now sells beer and wine, for example. "Used to be customers would come in and say, you have beer here?" She says, "I'd say, 'No, we a family store!'" Dukes continues, with preacherly emphasis, "Wal-Mart has a lot of power. But I believe in a God that has all power. We are a country that is founded on religious principles. And they should be enacted in every aspect of our lives, and it seems like my company is forgetting their religious principles, the religious principles that this *country*—as well as this *company*—was founded on."

The plaintiffs' involvement in the lawsuit has drawn mixed reactions from their pastors and fellow churchgoers. Dukes's crusade to reform Wal-Mart is inspired in large part by her role in her church. She made the decision to sue Wal-Mart when she realized, from conversations with her fellow ministers, "Since I preach the Gospel, I have to stand up against atrocities in society. You don't just look the other way and say, 'I don't want to get involved.'" She realized that if she took on Wal-Mart, she could encourage her congregation to fight injustice in their own lives. "Sometimes I say, 'That could be the only reason that you are born, to *participate* in that situation,'" she says. "My strength comes from my belief, and my faith in God. And I don't care how many lawyers [Wal-Mart] brings to the table. And I don't care how much moneybags, boxes and truckloads, that they have. It would not change my conviction. There are errors in Wal-Mart that need to be fixed." Arana, too, draws strength from her church and her faith. Her pastor supports her suit against Wal-Mart: she showed him a *Fortune* magazine article about it and "he thought it was awesome." Most importantly, she says, "I know the Lord has got my back." Indeed, like Dukes, Arana feels a special responsibility to take on Wal-Mart's discrimination because "I have the Lord to lean on, and other women may not have that."

Page, on the other hand, has met with hostility from members of her mostly white Tulsa, Oklahoma, church, who feel strong loyalty to Wal-Mart. Page's first job was as a teacher in a fundamentalist Christian school run by her parents in Virginia. Her family lives in Tulsa now because her sister moved there to attend Oral Roberts University, founded by the eponymous Evangelist. "Most of the church people are very judgmental. They look at you like you are a traitor," she says. "You're the evil one coming against a Christian company. They're like, 'You should let God handle that.'" One woman told Page, "When I have trouble at my job, I just pray on it."

Gunter does not have her church's blessing for participating in *Dukes v. Wal-Mart* either. She says some of her fellow churchgoers feel that suing Wal-Mart is "not the Christian thing to do." Her pastor has been "noncommittal. He said I needed to pray on it and do what I needed to do. He hasn't shed any light that what I'm doing is right."

Despite the outright falsehood of the company mythology when compared to reality, Wal-Mart has been tremendously successful at socializing employees into its culture, as the plaintiffs' experiences show. People believe in it, and want very badly to be a part of it. During the Wal-Mart cheers at the 2003 meeting, no one rolled her eyes, jeered, or expressed even the mildest skepticism. Of course, workers are selected to attend the annual meeting only if they have already shown a dedication to the company, but to the uninitiated observer, it still seems remarkable that so many Americans—normally reluctant to act collectively—would be willing to give over their individuality to engage in these Nurembergian rites.

As a visitor, I was reluctant to participate in the cheer, but didn't want to stand out by not joining in. One matronly

manager from New Mexico was sympathetic. "I was embarrassed to do the cheer at first. I used to hate it—I thought it
was so hokey!" She added apologetically, as one might if an
outsider had witnessed a bizarre family ritual of which one
was rather fond, "But now I love it."

Oddly, since Wal-Mart is notorious for its single-minded
devotion to profit, the Wal-Mart culture appeals to many
Americans' desire to believe in something more transcen-
dent than commerce. Arana describes how she felt about the
company when she first came to work at the Duarte store:
"It wasn't about how much they were going to pay. They had
values, and I thought, I can get with that." At the annual
meeting, the manager from New Mexico, a reasonable
woman clearly not given to groupthink, wouldn't stand up
for Amy Grant's ovation, and did not applaud any of the
mid-level executives. "Just being an entertainer is not enough
of a contribution," she said. "Neither is making money." But
when Tom Coughlin, then president and CEO of Wal-Mart
and Sam's Club, took the stage, she scrambled to her feet.
"For him I stand," she said.

It is no wonder that the Wal-Mart culture is the envy of
the business world. It is venerated as a model of cohesive-
ness and team spirit by the business press and by Harvard
Business School, where it is frequently used as a case study
on successful corporate culture. The Wal-Mart culture is
prominent in the lawsuit, not only because its bogus promises have angered women, but because Wal-Mart's success in creating such a cohesive culture undermines one of
the defense lawyers' central claims: that any discrimination

plaintiffs experienced was isolated, because every store is different. Store managers have so much independence, according to this argument, that it is impossible to make generalizations about company practices. This is the "every store an island" defense, one used frequently by corporate defense lawyers trying to shield their clients from liability for the behavior of "a couple knuckleheads."

William Bielby, a sociology professor at the University of California at Santa Barbara and the president of the American Sociological Association who is also an expert witness in *Dukes v. Wal-Mart*, argued in a report supporting the plaintiffs that the very success of Wal-Mart culture was precisely what made the pervasive discrimination so troubling. Bielby's academic specialty is gender discrimination, labor markets, and the personnel practices of organizations. He has testified in major sex discrimination class-action suits, against Lucky Stores and Publix, both of which were litigated by Brad Seligman, and against Home Depot.

Bielby based his report on material in depositions of Wal-Mart managers, as well as on internal memos, reports, presentations, and correspondence. He also relied on scholarship in the field, including his own. To test Wal-Mart's "every store an island" defense, the plaintiffs had asked Bielby to figure out whether the personnel system at Wal-Mart was essentially the same across its retail divisions. Bielby found that every Wal-Mart store was emphatically not an island, that in fact the company is unusually centralized and coordinated, and that its culture "sustains uniformity in policy and practice" throughout its operations. He found that this level of centralization and control extended to human resources practices, which were closely monitored by frequent store visits from regional and district management.

Citing Wal-Mart's famously uniform culture and the fact that it is held up as a model of such by the business world, Bielby concluded that it was sustained through ongoing training and "socialization," by relocating managers from store to store, and by promoting from within the company. Wal-Mart has many terms and expressions that are understood by nearly everyone in the organization and only by them. One example is the "Open Door," the idea that if employees have a complaint, they can take it to any level of the organization and it will be heard without repercussion. This notion is ridiculed by many workers, who describe it as the "Out the Door" policy because of the company's practice of firing complainers. Another piece of Wal–Mart-speak is the "Ten Foot Rule," meaning that if you come within ten feet of a customer, you have to say hello and ask if she needs help.

A great deal of other evidence unearthed in the course of the *Dukes* discovery process supports Bielby's analysis. Bentonville controls the temperature of the refrigerators in stores all over the country; if a manager in Alaska wants to turn up the temperature in his store, he needs to call someone in Arkansas and ask permission to do so. Wal-Mart workers interviewed for this book as well as those who have given testimony in Dukes tended to agree with Bielby that the company was very homogeneous throughout its operations and was highly centralized.

Many who had worked in more than one Wal-Mart location commented on the consistency of practices and language from store to store (though some people reported having a much better experience in one place than another, usually because they liked individual managers or coworkers better). "It has been my experience that they are pretty much the same," says Lorraine Hill, who worked for Wal-Mart in both Rock Springs, Wyoming, and Oxford, Maine. "Same rules, same theory, same intimidation. Same everything, and same low wages."

One particularly Orwellian example of Bentonville's control over stores occurred when the war on Iraq began in March 2003. The order came down from Arkansas that CNN's war coverage would be broadcast into the stores around the clock. Constance Hays reported in the *New York Times* on the mood in Wal-Mart stores near bases, where many employees and customers had family members in the Gulf: "The round-the-clock coverage was not well received at stores where the American forces represented real people, not just images on a screen. Under Wal-Mart policy, stores are not allowed to turn the monitors off, and because it is a closed system, they cannot change the channel to something else." A store manager complained, and by March 22, the televised war briefings were scaled back to two per day.[3]

Certainly this story is disturbing, yet a consistent corporate culture is not totalitarian and creepy by definition. Depending on the values it promotes, it could have positive potential. Plaintiffs rightly argue that with such centralized operations and such enthusiasm for team spirit, Wal-Mart would be well positioned to inculcate values of equality and to become a workplace in which sexism is not tolerated. Instead, sexism is a visible part of the company culture, even at the highest levels. Throughout 2002 and 2003, as *Dukes v. Wal-Mart* moved through the discovery process, this became more and more apparent. The plaintiffs charged that a degrading atmosphere in the stores is supported by company leadership's example.

In speeches to company managers, CEO Tom Coughlin has stressed the importance of winning the customer's trust. When the plaintiffs' attorney, Joe Sellers, deposed Coughlin, he showed Coughlin handwritten notes for such a speech, in which the CEO had written that customers should feel as if they could trust Wal-Mart employees with "their wife and their wallet." Coughlin admitted those notes were his own, and that he gave this speech frequently. Sellers said later that he found Coughlin's use of the term "wife" revealing, as it suggested that he assumed he was speaking to a predominantly male group and because "it sure came across that you were trusting them with your chattel, your property."

Rhonda Harper, a former vice president of marketing at Sam's Club, also gave provocative testimony about sexism in the corporate culture of Wal-Mart. Harper's salary was in the mid–200s, so hers was a more privileged perspective than that of most witnesses and plaintiffs, but one that offers great insight into the culture at the top and the attitudes of those who have the power to set the tone—and an example—for everyone else in the company. Harper was reluctant to testify because of an agreement she'd signed with the company, but the judge ruled that her obligation to obey a subpoena took precedence over her agreement with Wal-Mart. "The judge said I had to tell the truth, so here I am," she testified in her deposition.

Setting Wal-Mart in its context, Harper, who worked at headquarters, described Bentonville and the northwest Arkansas region as "a good ole boy environment. It is a culture that has been stable for many, many years. There hasn't been, as you would have in cosmopolitan areas, as much integration, diversity, differences expressed. Many of the people have lived there their entire lives." Many Wal-Mart officers "grew up together, went to school together, started out in the company together. . . which is one of the reasons why they're so successful, because it is a very close environment there."

Harper, who has an MBA from Emory University, is clearly sophisticated and well educated compared to many Wal-Mart executives, most of whom have not spent much time working in other companies or acquiring formal education. Harper and others have suggested that the company's rural, small-town northwest Arkansas roots may well contribute to the sexism in Wal-Mart's corporate culture. Yet the problem shouldn't be blamed on "the South," as many observers have been tempted to do. Gender disparities exist in Wal-Mart stores in every region. Besides, other southern companies have done relatively well in promoting women to the corporate level: according to Catalyst, an organization that tracks women's progress in the business world, 16.2 percent of the corporate officers in companies based in the South are women (the national average is 15.7 percent).

Rhonda Harper had tremendous promise, and Wal-Mart knew it. Before coming to Sam's Club she had worked in brand management at Kraft and in marketing at the American Red Cross, Nabisco, Vanity Fair Intimates, and other companies. Her name was known in the industry, and her award-winning work was widely recognized. She was recruited by Wal-Mart in 2000, and in March 2001, Wal-Mart's then CEO, Lee Scott, told her she was being groomed to become head of marketing for all of Wal-Mart within a few years.

In sharp contrast with many of the male executives at the company, Harper is articulate, her mind lively and critical. After a series of company-sponsored intelligence tests that was conducted by Personnel Decisions International (PDI), a Texas-based company, she was told she scored "in the top handful of [Wal-Mart] employees," including individuals at the highest levels—the CEO, for example—and was in the 99th percentile for people in any company holding a position similar to hers. After the PDI tests in late summer 2001, she says she was told by Dale Thompson, the vice president of PDI, "You could be the one," meaning she could eventually become the CEO of Wal-Mart.

Despite Harper's obvious potential, she was never able to succeed at Wal-Mart. Eventually, after being repeatedly reprimanded and reminded of the importance of "fitting in better with the Wal-Mart culture," in late 2001 she had a meeting which she describes as "abrupt... I remember Tom Grimm [then president and CEO of Sam's Club] looking at me and saying, 'Rhonda, it's over.'.... And I think that might have been the only thing he said." She was fired less than two months after the PDI consultant had said she might become the first female CEO of the company. (Since leaving Wal-Mart, she has moved to Marietta, Georgia, a suburb of Atlanta, and started her own marketing company, which made a profit in its very first year.)

Under questioning by plaintiffs' lawyers, Harper described behavior she witnessed at Wal-Mart. "In some cases it struck me as insensitive to individuals," she testified, particularly individuals who were women. "I found that somewhat ironic in a culture that was predicated on 'Respect for the Individual.'" Many hourly workers echoed Harper's observation. A black woman from Ohio who feels she suffered race and sex discrimination at Wal-Mart (she is not a plaintiff) said, "They always going on about respect for the individual. Where's it at?"

Wal-Mart's in-house training is overseen by the Walton Institute, based in Bentonville. Harper testified that in one training session at the Walton Institute she heard a store manager explain why there were no female managers in his store. Owing to child-care problems and the long hours required of managers, "He didn't think they would be able to perform the responsibilities Wal-Mart demanded." He thought that "they didn't fundamentally want it." As a mother with an extremely successful career, Harper found it unlikely that most women would be unable or unwilling to work management jobs simply because of child-care responsibilities.

Other attitudes Harper described were more ludicrous: "It wouldn't be abnormal" for senior management to refer to women working in the stores as "little Janie-Qs" and "girls."[4] She noted that "Janie-Q" was a "pet name for consumers as well as associates." Despite her objections, use of the term continued. Harper added dryly, "I believe... there would be some in the organization who would classify it as a term of endearment."

In a photo in a January 2001 issue of *Wally World*, the company newsletter, distributed to Wal-Mart workers, Jim Haworth, then the executive vice president of operations for Sam's Club, was shown sitting in a chair in the shape of a leopard-skin-covered spike heel. The photo was taken at a December 2000 holiday party for store employees, a party Harper remembered well. On another occasion, Harper saw Haworth onstage surrounded by women, some of whom were Wal-Mart associates, who were dancing and singing. Women were lining up to have their picture taken with Haworth—a ritual that was, according to Harper, very much part of company culture: "It was done year after year." (Haworth was promoted in July 2001 to executive vice president of operations for all of Wal-Mart.)

Harper also bristled at some of the recreation she was expected to take part in as a Wal-Mart executive, activities that she felt reflected the macho culture of Wal-Mart. One event she participated in was a quail-hunting expedition at the Walton family ranch in Texas, in February 2001. "Evidently that's the best time for quail," she remarked during her deposition. "Who knew?" Harper was one of only three women on the excursion, which was for about 30 of Wal-Mart's top officers.

The quail-hunting trip has been a cherished ritual in Wal-Mart culture since the company's founding. Sam Walton loved to hunt, and his family was accustomed to hosting Wal-Mart officers—many of whom hunted in northwest Arkansas—at the Texas ranch. "I thought it odd," Harper testified. "Actually, I thought it was a joke when they told me about it, quite frankly." During her fifteen months as a Wal-Mart officer, it was the company's only executive retreat. As she anticipated the excursion, "What went through my mind was, a ninety-thousand-acre ranch in Texas, you know, owned by the world's richest family, I'm thinking day spa." But just before they left, she realized her colleagues hadn't been kidding about the hunting: "They were serious, they were talking about snake guards. . . guns and shooting and all sorts of fun stuff." At the last minute, she went out and bought some hunting gear, realizing that "this isn't a corporate retreat. We're really going to go out there and kill things."

Julie Donovan, a *Dukes* witness, in an affidavit described a similarly macho culture at Wal-Mart headquarters. In 1996, when Donovan worked in the head office as a senior buyer, Ray Hobbs, a senior vice president, told Donovan that he was surprised that she, a woman, was in such a high position at Wal-Mart, and that it would be better if she were home raising children. During a performance evaluation during which they discussed her next move with the company, he "assured" her she shouldn't worry about trying to advance her career with Wal-Mart because "you aren't a part of the boy's club, and you should raise a family and stay in the kitchen." Hobbs also told her she did not play well with the "boys" at the company, and that because she didn't hunt or fish, she probably wouldn't advance any further. Informally—not through any written complaint or official use of the Open Door policy—she complained to her supervisor about the way she was being treated. He admonished her to "have a thick skin." Donovan also testified that in order to gain her male colleagues' respect, she had to focus conversations on hunting or sports.

"To be effective as an officer you need to be able to become part of the informal network," Rhonda Harper stated in her deposition, but this was difficult at Wal-Mart. "I didn't go fishing with them. I wondered if I had been able to do some of those things if I might have assimilated more quickly into the organization."

In 1995, Robert Reich, the Clinton administration's labor secretary, in the report of the Labor Department's Glass Ceiling Commission, *A Solid Investment: Making Full Use of the Nation's Capital,* mentioned the lack of access to "informal networks of communication" as a major barrier to women's advancement in corporate America. As examples of this, he cited casual conversations conducted during hunting trips, golf games, and "other pursuits not usually undertaken by women and people of color." The camaraderie established through these kinds of activities "can give white males a commanding advantage." Even in the advertising industry, where women and gay men are plentiful, shooting weekends are not unknown. As recently as June 2001—the month Dukes filed her suit—the *New York Times,* in an article exploring barriers

to women in corporate America, reported that women's exclusion from casual social and business relationships remained a problem and "the importance of male-bonding
events, like golf, can't be overestimated" in solidifying males'
advantages in the corporate world.[5] Golf remains controversial, as the fury over the Augusta Golf Club's sexist policies
showed; part of the reason women's groups were so agitated
by the Augusta Golf Club's exclusion of women is that golf
is still a popular bonding activity for businesspeople.

Rhonda Harper testified that once, when she was travel-
ing with a male officer, some store managers asked what it
was like being his secretary. This was probably a misunder-
standing and not a heinous act of sexism, but it indicates
that a female Wal-Mart executive was highly unusual and,
more disturbingly, for some in the company still unimagin-
able. On other business trips, Harper recalled, "I would be
the only [woman] on the corporate jet. . . . The pilots would
say, you know, 'Welcome gentlemen.'. . . I again don't know
if you would classify that as sexist or not, but clearly there I
was—I was sitting there." No one ever corrected the pilots
or said, "We're not all gentlemen here." Harper recalls, "I
would sometimes just go, 'And hello, ladies,' and there would
be laughter, you know."

She described a sales conference, attended by thousands
of store managers, with a football theme: "It was a very, in
my opinion, traditionally male theme." She brought that up
with her colleagues at headquarters, not because she thought
it was sexist but because all that male bonding seemed like a

distraction from focusing on the relationship with customers—the overwhelming majority of whom are women.

Of the particularly distasteful incidents at Wal-Mart—the "high heel thing"; Haworth's posing for pictures with a bevy of women; the airplane moment; the secretary comment; the references to Janie-Qs (all of which Harper discussed with her fellow officers)—Harper said she believed these incidents were "inappropriate or at the very least unusual," judging by her experience working for several other large corporations. It was "behavior that I would not anticipate existing in a corporate environment. . . I had never seen it before." She thought it was a real possibility that her Wal-Mart colleagues didn't know this kind of thing was inappropriate. "It is my nature to be very candid and direct," she testified. "I felt the need to bring [these concerns] forward because many of the folks who were at the officer level at Wal-Mart had never worked anywhere else."

Complaining about these incidents didn't help Harper make friends at Wal-Mart; neither did what many perceived as her haughty attitude. She just didn't fit in. Harper describes Wal-Mart headquarters as a cliquish atmosphere: "Either you're Wal-Mart, or you're everything else in the world." She attributes her problems at the company to the fact that she was an "outsider" who didn't conform to "the norm in the culture." The plaintiffs' lawyers asked Harper repeatedly whether her difficulties with Wal-Mart culture had to do with her gender; was she "different" because she was a woman? Harper was very careful not to exaggerate, not to blame her difficulties at the company solely on gender, and brought up examples of men who were also outsiders and had trouble fitting into Wal-Mart's insular culture. Eventually, however, she said, "I believe it has to do with who I am as a human being and one of my characteristics is that I am a woman." Her former boss, Celia Swanson, the Sam's Club executive vice president for membership, marketing, and administration—at that time the only woman among Wal-Mart's senior officers—put it more bluntly, testifying in her deposition that Harper hadn't learned "how to work around and manage the male ego."

The atmosphere Rhonda Harper describes thrives in a much cruder form at Wal-Mart's middle-management level and in the stores. Many managers show an appalling lack of respect for women, which sends a clear message about their place in the company. Melissa Howard, a store manager in Decatur, Indiana, testified that at the annual meeting in Fayetteville, male managers would go out to strip clubs together and that it was "an accepted part of the culture." Once, when a group of district and store managers were making a 16-hour drive from Decatur to Bentonville for a meeting (typical of Wal-Mart's tightfistedness, the company wouldn't spring for plane tickets for this 700-mile journey), the men stopped the car to take a break in a strip club. Howard didn't want to go in, but it was nighttime and she didn't think it would be safe to sit in the parking lot alone. At one point, one of the strippers approached Howard, and Kevin Washburn, a district manager, offered the dancer $50 to go "out back" and have a "threesome" with himself and a shocked Howard. On the way home from Bentonville, the men stopped at two more strip clubs while Howard and the one other female manager sat in the back and repeatedly asked to be taken back to the motel.

Howard's district manager sometimes held lunch meetings at Hooters restaurants. Howard, the only female store manager in her district, was "forced to listen to lots of discussion among the male managers about the waitresses' breasts and butts and which sexual experiences they would like to have with them. While it was humiliating to be there, I was reluctant to complain."

Hooters is an Atlanta-based nationwide sports bar and restaurant chain in which the customers, 70 percent of whom are male, are waited on by attractive and scantily clad "Hooters Girls" who wear color-coordinated sporty outfits displaying porn-star cleavage and shorts that are as brief as shorts can be without being underwear. The company's website features aphorisms such as "Men have different faces so you can tell them apart," and boasts that since the company's founding, "the Hooters concept has undergone very little change. . . understandable given the tremendous success the Hooters concept has enjoyed." The Hooters "concept" is women with big breasts, wearing very little clothing, serving men.

Actually, the company argues that its "concept" is *feminist*. The company waxes eloquent on Hooters Girls' "right to use their natural female sex appeal to earn a living. . . . To

Hooters, the women's rights movement is important because it guarantees women have the right to choose their own careers, be it a Supreme Court Justice or Hooters Girl."

Hooters is quite right that women have a right to use their sexuality to earn a living. But it is preposterous for any other company to hold business meetings at the restaurant chain, and it is easy to imagine the mortification of a female manager attempting to be taken seriously by—or simply to fit in with—her male colleagues as they ogle Hooters Girls, watch sports on TV, and bask comfortably in a made-for-males environment.

Probably many companies employ middle-management goofballs who don't realize that this sort of thing isn't acceptable. But Wal-Mart's vice president for human resources should. When *Dukes* lawyers took Coleman Peterson's deposition and asked him what he thought of the practices Melissa Howard described, he was quick to insist that get-togethers at strip clubs on company time were not "something Wal-Mart culture would support and believe is okay." Asked about business meetings at Hooters, however, Peterson, the chief human resources officer of the world's largest workforce, reserved judgment. "It is conceivable in some small town that Hooters is kind of like the restaurant *du jour*, okay," he testified, "and that it is viewed as one of the most elegant and really one of the best places to meet and eat." In other words, it is perfectly okay to subject female employees to Hooters if it is the best restaurant in town. Joe Sellers later scoffed at this notion: "I don't even know if they serve food."

In Peterson's defense, Hooters does serve food. Indeed, one of its mottoes is "You can sell the sizzle, but you have to deliver the steak." Mike McNeil, a Hooters spokesman, did not think a Hooters restaurant would be an outlandish spot for an informal business meeting, although it has no conference or banquet rooms. But even McNeil seemed amused when told about Peterson's assertion that Hooters was sometimes the "most elegant and best place" around. "I was not aware of that [testimony]," he said, "but bless him whoever said that. We appreciate that. It's kinda like, in the eye of the beholder." Pausing to consider the possibilities, the flack said, "Wal-Mart is in a lot of small towns. So if you were in some place like Muskegon, Michigan, or Dothan, Alabama, that statement might actually be true."

The "knuckleheads" Melissa Howard worked with are hardly unique. At least the strippers she encountered weren't on store property. Angela Horton, a team leader in a Sam's Club in Onalaska, Wisconsin, testified that a company-sanctioned "Spirit Committee" hired a stripper to perform at her store's mandatory morning employee meeting, to celebrate a male store manager's birthday. The women who complained about this were called "a bunch of whiners."

In the stores, as at headquarters, "informal networks" pose obstacles to women's advancement. As an assistant manager in Indiana, Howard was often left to run the store by herself while the general manager went off and socialized with male employees—playing pool, going out to lunch, drinking together, and going to the race track. Other women have complained that managers play golf with male employees and don't befriend women or ask them to lunch. (Wal-Mart's anti-fraternization rules do prohibit managers from socializing with workers they supervise, but many workers say that this rule is often violated, to the advantage of men.) Numerous women have testified that an "old boy network" of friend-ships among men in the stores helps men to be promoted more quickly than women.

Despite the broken promises, the democratic mythologies of the Wal-Mart culture are so compelling that even women who have been badly burned by the company still want to believe in it. They tend to make sense of the company's be-trayals with a "golden age" story. In this narrative, Wal-Mart was a good company for all workers, men and women, back in Sam Walton's day. Now that he's dead, things have changed. Indeed, one of the remarks most often made by Wal-Mart workers who are now dissatisfied with the com-pany is, "If Sam Walton could see his company now, he'd be turning over in his grave." This devotion to Walton is not necessarily rational. As is well documented in Bob Ortega's *In Sam We Trust* as well as in Walton's own autobiography, the company founder was aware of the barriers women faced in the company and did little to remove them. He was also a cheapskate, adamantly devoted to the bottom line, and viru-lently anti-union. That the company, in its relentless expan-sion, has become a hellish and impersonal place to work should be seen as consistent with "Mr. Sam's" values.

Yet most employees' view of Walton as a benevolent founder, and Wal-Mart as an essentially good company is unwavering. Betty Dukes says that when Walton was alive, the company had "seeds of religious respect for the family but that's all eroded. Like the 'Wal-Mart family,' it's disappearing like the dinosaurs." Joyce Moody, a witness in *Dukes* who worked for Wal-Mart for more than two decades beginning as a young woman in Mississippi, agrees. Many changes in the company have contributed to her anger about the sex discrimination. When Wal-Mart lost much that was appealing about its culture, its exploitative and often unfair practices became apparent to many more workers. "It's not the same company that it was in the earlier days," Moody says.

"The women that I worked with throughout the years, we always knew that the guys made more than we did," she continues. "But back in those early days, you didn't hear so much about discrimination, or equality, or anything like that." She acknowledges that this had something to do with the larger culture; she was in the Deep South, where feminist concepts have been slow to penetrate everyday conversation. But even more saliently, she says, "A lot of people were happy with Wal-Mart at that time and I don't think anyone would have ever thought about bringing any charges against the company. Because you did have that family atmosphere. When I first started, it was a good company to work for. The associates in the store, they were not only coworkers—they were friends. We attended weddings and funerals and baby showers."

Like many other workers, Moody says the company lost that "community spirit" as it grew bigger, and especially "after Mr. Sam died." Many managers came into the company who "didn't understand Wal-Mart culture. To me the associates were the backbone of the company," she says, "but then it turned to management." In earlier times the employees had a sense that their opinion mattered, but in her later years at the company, "the associates weren't listened to as well as in the earlier days." For example, Wal-Mart had long had a tradition of holding "grassroots" meetings to find out what employees' concerns are, and to get their ideas about how the business could be improved. These meetings embodied Wal-Mart's notion that workers mattered: an employee could raise any issue she liked in the "grassroots" meeting. But in recent years, Moody says, the company has become so top-down that employees are now "told what they were going to be able to discuss in the grassroots."

Many long-term employees involved in the *Dukes* lawsuit agree with Moody's description of a breakdown in Wal-Mart's populist culture. Kathleen MacDonald, a *Dukes* witness still working at the Aiken, South Carolina, Wal-Mart, says, "The day Sam died was the day Wal-Mart joined corporate America. Things changed drastically. Not only for women but for all employees." MacDonald cites the content of employees' mandatory morning meetings. When Sam Walton was alive, meetings consisted of "discussions of how we were feeling, national events, what was happening around the company, and announcements of employee weddings, sickness. Then they would make a statement about sales, but it would just be a short statement." Employee input was solicited on a wide range of issues. But after Walton's death, "Our morning meetings were filled with how much our sales increased in different departments, or what we were expected to accomplish and get done that week. The personable comments were put to a minimum, our ideas no longer respected. The way we felt about things was no longer considered."

In the early days, she continues, "We were one big happy family. We looked out for one another." If someone in an employee's family died, "the store manager would attend the service and he would get a list of people to bring food to the house and would comfort and do whatever he had to for that person." If an employee called in sick, the manager would, in all sincerity, say something like, "Oh, I'm so sorry. I hope you get better." Then Mr. Sam died. Kathleen notes that "they didn't even close the store" to observe his death, even though workers felt so strongly about him. "One month later, we were informed that we were going to build a Supercenter that sold groceries and it was going to be wonderful. The store then changed its hours to be open 24 hours. Before moving to the new location they made us turn in our smocks." The old smocks bore the slogan "Our People Make the Difference." The new ones emphasize quite a different idea: "How May I Help You?"

MacDonald relates an incident that she feels sharply underscores the difference between the old Wal-Mart and the new. Recently, a worker in the Aiken store died, a woman who had been with the company for 17 years. "In the morning meeting the store manager said, 'Well, we have suffered a loss, but we have a business to run, business as usual. Do you all want to do a Wal-Mart cheer?'"

Dee Gunter, speaking of the decline in Wal-Mart culture, says, "That can happen in any business: the parents found it, then the kids take it over and it goes to pieces." Of Sam Walton's daughter, Alice, who is not at all involved in the day-to-day operations of Wal-Mart, Gunter says, "She's the third-richest woman in the world. She can sit back while we're treated like slaves. Why did she step so far from what her parents believed in? What's she going to do with all that money?" (Alice and her mother, Helen, are tied for fourth place in *Forbes* magazine's 2003 roundup of the world's richest individuals; they are the only two women among the top ten.) Sam Walton worked hard to build Wal-Mart, says Dukes. "But his sons Rob, Bob, whatever their names might be, they're not [traveling] around the country, they're not working overnights. No, they're living the good life. It seems they have forgotten what made Wal-Mart so great: Ordinary people."

Steve Jenkins is a labor organizer in New York City who has worked extensively with immigrants in Brooklyn garment factories. He says it is common for employees in family businesses to idealize the father-founder and to vilify the sons who take over. Regardless of the facts, workers tend to blame the ruthlessness of the business on the founders' shiftless sons. "They always think the son is a jerk," Jenkins says and points out that the founder is usually closer to the workers in his class origins; he may be better able to relate to them culturally and, whatever the material reality, better able to nourish the impression that he cares. His heirs have been raised in privilege, and are thus easy targets for employee resentment. In fact, Rob Walton *is* slick and expensively dressed, has no regional accent, and conveys none of his father's folksy manner.

Despite everything they've suffered, many *Dukes* plaintiffs still believe in the Wal-Mart culture. Stephanie Odle has kept her Sam Walton pin, even though the back is rusted—"I took it out just the other day." If the *Dukes* plaintiffs win, she would be happy to return to work for Wal-Mart. "[Wal-Mart] can be the company that they were when I started working for them," she insists. "I believe in that company."

3

"AN EXCEPTIONAL WOMAN": (NON)PROMOTIONS AT WAL-MART

THE PROMISES OF the Wal-Mart culture ring especially hollow to women who have been unfairly denied advancement, women like Christine Kwapnoski, who worked at Sam's Club for 15 years before getting a promotion. Wal-Mart's failure to promote them into management positions is, for women who so fully bought into the Wal-Mart promise of working-class mobility, one of the company's worst betrayals.

A dedicated company woman, Kwapnoski speaks Sam's Club jargon so fluently it is sometimes difficult for a company outsider to understand what she is talking about; her conversation is peppered with phrases like "Ten-key" and "stock status." Her talents are so obvious from conversation with her that Michael Gray, one of Wal-Mart's lawyers on *Dukes*, deposing her before her last promotion, admitted to plaintiffs' attorney Betty Lawrence that it was clear that Kwapnoski "should be in management."[1]

Kwapnoski began working at Sam's in 1986, in Grand-view, Missouri. It was her first real job "besides fast food." She learned quickly and her evaluations were effusively complimentary. Hired as a cashier, she moved quickly to the claims office, where she was a recognized expert; workers in Sam's Clubs throughout the region would call her for advice. "I was the go-to person," she recalls, "before they called the help desk or the Home Office or anything."

She began telling her managers that she wanted to be promoted, but no one told her what she needed to do to qualify for management training, or how she might apply. Job openings were never posted; male coworkers were moved into jobs before Kwapnoski even had a chance to express interest.

In 1993 she finally saw a posted opportunity. Wal-Mart had just bought Pace, a warehouse chain previously owned by K-Mart, and was going to convert the Pace stores into Sam's Clubs. The company needed a Sam's Club associate to go to California on a temporary mission to teach the Pace employees about Sam's Club culture and practices. Kwapnoski applied, and was selected to go.

Once there, she did such a good job of turning the Pace store into a Wal-Mart and training its workers in the Wal-Mart way of life that she was offered a full-time position in Concord, California. She accepted, with no idea of the move's terrible price. Divorced, she had two young children,

Tiffany and Zachary, whom she intended to bring to California. But while she was in California looking for permanent housing, her ex-husband accused her of abandoning the children, and a family court judge took his side. She lost custody, and her children, Tiffany and Zachary, now live with her only during the summer and the Christmas holiday season.

Despite this wrenching family ordeal, Kwapnoski continued to work hard and earned praise for her performance, which was also acknowledged by merit raises. For the next seven years, she worked on the dock, in the receiving area, in the freezer-cooler, and in the auditing department. She was always available for any positions she had to fill, and was always willing to take on extra tasks, even if they weren't in her job description. "I've never let something suffer just because it wasn't my job," she says. "I've always stepped up and done that little extra. Why, I'm not sure. But I do. . . I guess I always step up to the challenge of doing something well. A little bit crazy? Worked at Sam's long enough to be certifiable."

Kwapnoski was sure she would eventually be rewarded with a promotion. She frequently told her managers— "every assistant manager and general manager that's ever been over me," plus the district operations manager—that she wanted to become a team leader, an hourly supervisory position, and eventually an area manager. These positions, which were never posted, were given to men less qualified than Kwapnoski, and she often had to train them. Several of those men now work at Old Navy. "Oh my god, Old Navy!"

she says with a sigh. "I don't shop there because I'll run into them."

Kwapnoski worked on the dock, where boxes are unloaded, for several years during the 1990s. She often told her immediate superior, the dock lead Clark Holt, that she wanted to inherit his job when he moved on. She told the general manager, Alan Oshier, as well as assistant managers that she wanted the dock lead position. She knew she could do Holt's job well, and she felt it would help her advance in the company. But when Holt left the job, Oshier gave it to a man. Indeed, the dock lead position opened up several times throughout the 1990s, and although Kwapnoski was always the worker with the most experience on the dock, the job was always given to men.

After working on the dock, Kwapnoski worked in the freezer-cooler, and here, too, she sought to become a team leader and get ahead, and again—four times—she was passed over, each time for a less-qualified man. Finally, when there were no men left to take the position, management abolished the freezer-cooler team lead job title—though not the function itself. Then Kwapnoski "had all the responsibilities of that job without having the title or getting the pay raise for it."

Every time she asked to be promoted, Kwapnoski would get a different answer, but always the message was clear: not yet. "It was, 'You gotta do this, you gotta do that.' And I'd say, 'But I've done this, and I've done that!'" Like most women who have made it to Wal-Mart management, Kwapnoski is tough. She does not cry when recounting her Wal-Mart experiences, as many workers do; recalling something particularly heinous, she'll often pause and remark, with quiet sarcasm, "It was interesting." But it is clear she is still seething at her treatment.

Since job openings often weren't posted, Kwapnoski had to rely on the Sam's Club grapevine to learn about them. Men, however, had more access to the grapevine than she did since they were more likely to hang out with male managers. Nancy Hom, a *Dukes v. Wal-Mart* witness who worked as an assistant manager in the Concord, California, Sam's Club, testified that even when jobs were posted, the general manager had already decided whom he wanted to hire.

Hom, who testified that Kwapnoski was an "excellent employee," said that Kwapnoski had been qualified for the receiving area management position for several years, and had repeatedly been passed over for the position. Hom had recommended several times that Kwapnoski be promoted, to no avail.

Finally, in 1999, Kwapnoski became a team leader, a position she'd long viewed as a stepping stone to a management position. In June 2001, she was promoted again, becoming an area manager for the receiving department, one of the company's highest-level hourly supervisory jobs, two weeks after *Dukes* was filed and 15 years after she first started seeking a promotion into management. "It came as quite a shock to me because I had already been told there were two men who were more qualified," she says. Asked about their qualifications, she laughs. "They were males!" At the time she was not a plaintiff and had not yet heard about the lawsuit, but she now thinks the timing was not accidental.

After this promotion, the store's general manager, Alan Oshier, took every opportunity to belittle her, telling her to "doll up" and "dust the cobwebs off" her makeup. She laughs at that, observing that her job is hot and messy and involves almost no contact with the public. "I get dirty. I'm usually head over heels in a box counting something. I'm not gonna be in a skirt. I'm not gonna be in high heels."

Oshier told Kwapnoski she needed to be an area manager for a year before she could enter the management training program, which is required to become an assistant manager, a salaried position. She had never heard of a male worker having to fulfill this requirement. In fact, there are very few rules about how much experience a Sam's Club worker must have to enter the management training program. Kwapnoski had seen many male associates begin their Sam's Clubs careers in management training, without having to work any hourly jobs. After she'd been an area manager for a year, still eager to become an assistant manager, Kwapnoski asked Oshier again how she could get into management training. He suggested she keep doing what she was doing, and perhaps work as area manager in another part of the store to get more experience. Again, Kwapnoski had never heard of a man at Sam's Club being held to such a requirement.

Other women at the Concord store heard about the *Dukes* lawsuit. Knowing what Kwapnoski had experienced over the years in her efforts to be promoted, they encouraged her to come forward, and she became a plaintiff in the case. Though she'd been fully aware that Sam's Club was discriminating against her, she had never given much thought to feminism or workers' rights and was surprised to find herself taking a controversial public position. An individualist who does not believe in unions (at least, as many Wal-Mart people say, "not for this company"), Kwapnoski does not instinctively think collectively. Still, she now hopes intensely that her experience will help other women.

In the summer of 2002, Kwapnoski began trying to win back custody of her children, and didn't want to move away from Concord until the family court case was resolved. Before that she had always been available to relocate, and had never been told it was a requirement for becoming an assistant manager. Kwapnoski knew several male managers who'd been promoted to management without having to relocate. Now, Oshier was telling her that being available to move was an absolute prerequisite for the management training program. Once again, her promotion was stalled.

In January 2003, Kwapnoski had a chance encounter with a former colleague, Greg Johnston, with whom she'd worked in Missouri a decade before when she had been a cash-office associate and he had been an hourly supervisor. It was strange to run into him, and she couldn't help feeling the difference in their circumstances. While she had not even been promoted to the bottom rung of management, Johnston was now a regional vice president. "My former co-worker had risen to one of the highest positions at Sam's Club," she later testified. Still, it was good to see an old friend. Laughing, they recalled the time she began going into labor at work, nearly giving birth in the Sam's Club cash office. They gossiped about people they both knew from Missouri. Johnston asked her how things were going in California. She recalls saying, "You got time?" She told him the entire saga of her attempts to enter Sam's Club's management training program, knowing that he was in a position to help her. Johnston, who remembered her as an excellent worker, was sympathetic.

Not long after this conversation, Betty Lawrence, Kwapnoski's lawyer, deposed Johnston as part of the *Dukes* discovery process, and let him know that his old friend hadn't yet been promoted. He seemed surprised, as if he thought he'd taken care of the problem. Soon afterward Kwapnoski was at last allowed to enter the management training program. Once again, the lawsuit proved to be a boon to her career. Suddenly, the relocation requirement—indeed, all the odd criteria her managers had been inventing—didn't matter anymore. She is now an assistant manager over the bakery, and recently got a call from the regional personnel manager congratulating her on her outstanding sales numbers. Despite these personal successes, she has no intention of dropping out of the lawsuit.

Kwapnoski is not alone in struggling to be promoted at Wal-Mart. Many women have worked for years without getting the recognition they deserve, watching as men are promoted over them. At Wal-Mart, the lower a job's status and the worse it pays, the more women hold it. The lowest-paid workers are cashiers, and 92.5 percent of them are women. Most hourly supervisors—nearly 90 percent of customer service managers and 78 percent of department managers—

are women. The percentage of women declines the further up the hierarchy one advances: just over 40 percent of workers in the management trainee program are women, but women comprise only 14 percent of store managers. Only 10 percent of district managers and regional vice presidents are women.[2] The percentage of female hourly workers is nearly double the percentage of female salaried workers. Furthermore, though nearly 70 percent of the company's workforce is female, just one third of its salaried managers are women.

Marc Bendick, the labor economist whose report back in June 2001 had encouraged Brad Seligman to proceed with the suit, brought out a revised report in January 2003 that was even stronger than his first, because it included more up-to-date data and some new evidence.[3] Bendick was able to use some of Wal-Mart's own internal memos and reports, which gave him a much more rounded picture of the discussions about the gender issue within the company.

Although Wal-Mart had argued that comparisons to other firms are not relevant, Bendick pointed to an internal memo, distributed among all division heads in March 1999, in which the company compared itself to five of its competitors: CompUSA, Dayton Hudson (Target's parent company at that time), Home Depot, May Department Stores, and Toys R Us. Wal-Mart concluded that its percentage of women in management (32.4 percent) was "significantly behind several of the other retailers reporting (43.2 percent to 65.3 percent)." Looking at data collected by the national Equal Employment Opportunity Commission (EEOC) data (all companies are required to report personnel statistics to the government agency), the company concluded, in the same memo: "Our Wal-Mart percent of women trails both the retail industry and workforce averages. . . ." Obviously, in 1999 Wal-Mart thought that comparison to other firms was relevant, and was concerned about what the comparison showed, whatever the company's counsel might be arguing now.

Bendick refined what Wal-Mart already knew about itself, and confirmed it much more precisely. He compared the retailer to 20 competitors instead of only 5, put the stores in a category separate from other operations (such as corporate headquarters or distribution centers), and ran comparisons within 375 local labor markets, rather than simply comparing national averages.

For every year he looked at he found a significant difference between Wal-Mart's percentage of female managers and that of its competitors' within these local labor markets, and this was pretty stable throughout the 25-year period. Bendick's notion of "shortfall" was that if other retail chains were able to promote women into management, it meant women in that region were available, qualified, and willing to hold managerial positions. Bendick found that nationwide, the gaps between Wal-Mart's and its competitors' percentage of women in management were closing, but slowly—so slowly that, Bendick predicted, at this rate it would take Wal-Mart about 88 years to catch up with the competition.

Wal-Mart operates stores in all 50 states (though not in the District of Columbia). It would be tempting to attribute the shortfall entirely to the company's operation in rural, conservative, and southern areas—places where women might be more traditional in their desires. No doubt the sexism in company culture is related in part to its early growth in rural areas and small towns, and to the location of its headquarters in northwest Arkansas. But obviously that's not the whole story: Bendick found a shortfall in salaried women managers in four out of five Wal-Mart stores when compared to their local competitors—much too broad a pattern to be attributable to geography or regional culture. He also found a shortfall in Wal-Mart stores in 49 out of 50 states. (The one state in which Bendick did not find a statewide shortfall in the percentage of female managers was Vermont, which at that time had only three Wal-Mart stores—and there was a shortfall in two out of those three stores.)

Bendick found this shortfall not only in Wal-Mart's stores and headquarters, but also in the company's distribution centers, warehouses, administrative facilities, and other professional and blue-collar operations. This suggested to him that the lack of female managers reflected "company-wide corporate culture and attitudes, perceptions, policies, and practices that embody that culture."

In a June 2000 meeting in Bentonville, Coleman Peterson, then the head of the People Division, alerted his colleagues to Wal-Mart's "female trouble," mentioning that 52 percent of Target's managers were women compared to 33 percent of Wal-Mart's. He made similar statements in board meetings, according to the minutes of those meetings. In fact, throughout his tenure at Wal-Mart, Peterson, who retired in February 2004, repeatedly let his colleagues know that women were underrepresented in company management and offered suggestions on remedying the problem, including the idea of hiring a point person to oversee diversity initiatives.

When Joe Sellers deposed Peterson, he asked the People Division head about the comments he had made in June 2000. Peterson claimed that Target was including data from its department stores as well as its discount stores. He also claimed that department stores include department managers in management in their EEOC reporting, which Wal-Mart does not do. "Had we put department managers in those numbers," he testified, "we would be almost without exception better than every last one of the retailers. . . [listed] here."

Wal-Mart has consistently made this argument in its defense: competitors' numbers only look better because, when reporting personnel data to the EEOC, those competitors count department managers and other supervisors who are paid by the hour as managers, whereas Wal-Mart counts only salaried supervisors as managers. Peterson claimed that when he raised the issue of female representation at meetings and cited other companies' statistics, he always added this disclaimer about the hourly managers. If he did make such a point, it never appeared in the minutes of the meetings, a fact that Peterson was unable to explain.

Wal-Mart does have plenty of female department managers. In fact, the majority of hourly supervisors are women, as are the majority of other hourly workers at Wal-Mart. But few companies would define any workers who are paid an hourly wage as "managers." They are paid an hourly wage, not a salary, and they make significantly less money than salaried managers. A woman working as an hourly department manager makes on average $21,709 a year, whereas an assistant manager, the lowest level of salaried management, makes on average $37,322. Department managers also don't have what most companies would recognize as managerial responsibilities: they can't fire people and they can't give raises.

In any case, Peterson's claim that other retailers count department managers as managers didn't hold up under questioning. Peterson, who worked for the May Company, a department store, for 16 years, claimed that May counts wage-earning department managers as salaried managers in its EEOC reporting. Peterson also based his contentions on conversations he had had with his counterparts at Target, K-Mart, and Home Depot. When pressed, however, he admitted that he could not say for certain what these companies' reporting practices were.

In his revised report, Bendick ignored Peterson's dissembling and backpedaling, focusing instead on the essence of his claim. Using the EEOC data for Wal-Mart and 20 competitors, he compared the number of "managers" per comparable-sized store. Reasoning that every large retail store has more lower-level hourly supervisors than salaried managers, he figured that companies that counted department managers as managers would have a much larger number of managers. Looking at the stores' numbers, Bendick could find only a few that had so many "managers" that in order to achieve these numbers they must have been counting hourly supervisors. Wal-Mart had almost exactly the same number as the average: just a little over ten.

Furthermore, Bendick pointed out, Peterson's statement on how well Wal-Mart would do if department managers were counted as managers "is equivalent to a frank concession by Mr. Peterson that Wal-Mart's employment exhibits a very strong 'glass ceiling' for women at the department manager level."[4] The very definition of a glass ceiling, Bendick writes, is a "sharp decrease in the representation of women from one level in a hierarchy to the next one up."

This is not the only issue around which Peterson had to perform a complex dance as he made excuses for the company while at the same time trying to change it from within.

In a March 2002 memo to his home office colleagues, Peterson complained that Wal-Mart did not hold managers accountable for promoting more women and minority men. Under questioning from Sellers, Peterson distanced himself from the implied criticism in his statement, attributing it to a general spirit of perfectionism at the company. At Wal-Mart, he said, whatever the topic of conversation, the message sent by leadership is that "we can always do better." Pressed further, he said, "Part of my responsibility is to get everybody's attention."

Sellers, referring to the statement in the memo about not holding managers accountable, asked, "Well, was it a lie? Were you writing something that wasn't true?" Peterson, falling on his sword and impugning his own integrity to protect the company, answered, "Yes, I was." Of course, if

Dukes were to go to trial, Sellers would ask Peterson why the court should believe anything he says, since he admits lying to his own colleagues.

As Kwapnoski found out, if a woman does get promoted at Wal-Mart, it will take her much longer than her male counterparts. To become an assistant manager takes women on average 4.38 years and men less than 3 years. The few women who become store managers take, on average, more than 10 years to get there, but men just 8.64 years.[5] After seven years at Wal-Mart, Betty Dukes was still a cashier, yet she saw men who were new to Wal-Mart promoted into the management training program within the year. "They just rise from obscurity, up to the top. . . . How are they doing it so accelerated?" she wonders. "I have seen green straws come in, and become assistant manager, when they could not even find the cash register."

Richard Drogin, emeritus professor of statistics at California State University at Hayward and a private statistical consultant who was hired by the plaintiffs, found that these status gaps persisted despite women's lower turnover rates. In his February 2003 report, "Statistical Analysis of Gender Patterns in Wal-Mart Workforce," he reported that women remain at Wal-Mart much longer than men do. The average woman working full-time at Wal-Mart has been there for nearly 4.5 years, while her male counterpart has worked there for only 3.13 years. Even women working there part-time have been there longer than their male part-time colleagues. In 97 percent of Wal-Mart jobs, women have been working in those positions at the company longer than men.

Women also have higher performance ratings than men. Among hourly workers in 2001, women's performance ratings were higher overall than those of men, and for the major hourly positions—sales associates, cashiers, department managers—women scored higher than men. Much of the time, companies defend themselves against such dismal statistics by finding some way to argue that women are really not interested in management jobs. Company lawyers are essentially sticking to this tired argument (even though some Wal-Mart officials, under questioning from plaintiffs' lawyers, have waffled on this issue). Many women prefer the hourly jobs, Wal-Mart claims, because they have children and these jobs are more flexible. The department-manager job, an hourly supervisory position often held by women, works well for women with school-aged children because it is a weekday, daytime shift that usually ends in the late afternoon, whereas many salaried managers must work nights and weekends. Wal-Mart's lawyers argue that fewer women than men apply for management jobs, and that's why more men are hired. In fact, they point out, women are selected for such positions at a higher rate than they apply: 46 percent of support-manager applications were from women, and 47 percent of successful candidates were women. Twelve percent of store-manager applicants are women, whereas 16 percent of those selected are female.

Plaintiffs contend that the applicant pool does not reflect the true number of women interested in getting ahead at Wal-Mart, because in addition to a sexist company culture, so many of Wal-Mart's policies and practices discourage women from applying for promotions in the first place.

One of those, say plaintiffs, is the lack of job postings, which certainly held Kwapnoski back. Numerous other women have reported the same problem in their stores. Of her Pittsburg, California, Wal-Mart, Dukes says, "There was no posting that was set out, that you could see and inquire about. Nothing like that. I didn't know how they did things except I know you would hear, 'Oh, so and so's the department manager of this now.' I didn't know the in-between of it. Someone left and the next thing you know, someone had it."

Human resources experts agree that posting notices announcing job openings in places where employees can see them—break rooms, for example—tends to undermine favoritism and prejudice. Without postings, people friendly with management hear about opportunities—and no one else does. In a company like Wal-Mart, in which most managers are men, the people most likely to be friendly with management are, of course, other men. "They're buddies," says Dukes. "They drink together."

In his December 2002 deposition, Peterson admitted to Sellers that posting salaried job openings leads to greater equality of opportunity, reducing litigation by affecting "the fairness of how people get picked for jobs." He clarified that when jobs are posted, "People understand where the jobs are and they understand what it is you need to do to qualify for the jobs." Peterson acknowledged that Wal-Mart doesn't enforce job posting in any systematic way. Despite his belief in the importance of this practice, when asked about individual store managers' decisions not to post particular positions, Peterson said, "Frankly, it's not something I would look at or review." Nor, he added, would any of his staff in the People Division monitor this.

Experts who reviewed Wal-Mart's posting system found that Peterson was right—it wasn't much of a system. Experts hired by Wal-Mart found that before 2003, management trainee openings were not posted, though 95 percent of store-manager jobs were. William Bielby, the plaintiffs' sex discrimination expert, found that positions of comanager (second-in-command to the store manager) and assistant manager were rarely posted. The last is particularly significant because it is an entry-level management job, the one that an hourly supervisor is most likely to be promoted into. At Sam's Club, few management positions of any rank were posted. Bielby found that Wal-Mart had begun a system of computerized posting only in the late 1990s. Before that the company had used printed postings for some positions; there were no guidelines governing posting and no monitoring of job posting practice, and store managers had the authority to opt not to post an open position.

It has been difficult to figure out why job posting was so erratic at Wal-Mart. One obvious reason is that it does little if anything to boost profits, and it requires a sustained commitment to equality. Peterson testified that there are many managers in the stores who dislike "administrative processes." Although he has long been an advocate of job posting, he didn't appear to have much support for this stance either in the field or from the operations executives who have more power than he to enforce new policies.

In general, says Sellers, where hiring and promotions are concerned, Wal-Mart stores are managers' "little fiefdoms and they can do as they wish." Although Peterson was clearly concerned about women and minorities at the company, he had little authority to make or enforce new policies. According to Sellers,

> One of the schisms in this company, and it's true in many big companies. . . is that the operations people who generate the income are disdainful of the HR [human resources] people who don't generate income. . . . It's very hard given the mere fact that the operations people bring in the money and the human resources people expend money. . . . The operations people tend to be unreceptive to most of the things that the HR people recommend, and the HR people are. . . often rather meek and apologetic for the things they say, and pull their punches when it comes to saying what they really think. . . . It even leads companies, and this one is no exception, to refrain from bringing in people who are real assertive HR people because they'll be a nuisance. . . .[T]he entire attitude toward the HR process. . . [is] going to have to change.

Many witnesses have testified that men don't formally apply for their promotions; rather, they are tapped or groomed for their positions by managers who like them. One of those witnesses was Kenneth Christensen, a man who got his job in just that way. Christensen was the only male Wal-Mart employee to give a formal statement in support of the *Dukes* plaintiffs. Hired as a service technician in the Tire and Lube Express department in the Port Charlotte, Florida, Supercenter, Christensen was promoted after a few months. His store manager, a fellow with the unlikely name of Cary Grant, asked him if he wanted to become a service manager. "The position was not posted, and I did not have to formally apply or interview," said Christensen. "I merely had to accept the offer, and I was promoted."

An equally serious obstacle for women is the one that Sam Walton identified back in 1992: the relocation requirement. Wal-Mart's business rationale for that rule was that employees might find it awkward to be managed by coworkers who had previously occupied the same position in the hierarchy, and might not respect their authority. Not only Walton but also many other Wal-Mart officials have realized that the policy harms women and disrupts all employees' family lives, and that these concerns potentially outweighed questions of store politics. Until *Dukes v. Wal-Mart*, however, little changed.

Frances Jackson, a *Dukes* witness who has worked in an Aberdeen, North Carolina, Wal-Mart since 1987, is raising her grandchildren and caring for her ailing husband. She has often been told that she can't be promoted because she does not want to relocate her family. Women who are not involved in *Dukes* tell similar stories. One African American jewelry department manager in Ohio (she did not want to give her name), when asked about becoming a salaried manager, said, "They took the option away from me years ago. It was discrimination, I know for a fact." In order to go into management, she says, "they told me I would have to move. My husband was fine with moving as long as he could get a job that paid the same. He's behind me." But since her husband has a unionized job and makes more money than she does, the family had to be careful to move someplace where his opportunities would be decent. When she asked her managers where they'd be sending her, they couldn't say. They discouraged her, suggesting, "Maybe you shouldn't do it if you're so concerned about moving."

Moving clearly is a problem for many women. But Bielby noted that managers, thinking stereotypically, often wrongly assume that women are unable to relocate because of family commitments. This happens even to women who are undaunted by a relocation requirement. When Phyllis Lehman, a *Dukes* witness, was foods department manager in Liberty, Missouri, she repeatedly told her assistant manager that she wanted to be promoted into the management training program, even pointing out that if she were male she'd already be a salaried manager. He repeatedly reminded her that she'd have to move, with her children. She assured him—often—that she was perfectly willing to do just that, but to no avail. After several years of such exchanges, Lehman told her district manager she wanted to be promoted. Once again he reminded her she'd have to move, and that such a move would be difficult with children; he told her to go home and ask her children how they felt about moving. In her class-member declaration for the *Dukes* plaintiffs, she stated,

I felt like Mr. Schneider's response to my interest was not sincere, but I did go home and talk to my children. About a month later I was finally able to track down Mr. Schneider again and I let him know that my family was supportive of the move. Again he responded that he thought the move would be hard on my kids, but he said he would see what he could do. I never heard from him again about it.

Micki Miller Earwood, one of the original *Dukes* plaintiffs, worked in Urbana, Ohio. Her performance evaluations were usually excellent and almost always above average, so she wasn't surprised when, in 1998, her district manager, Cindy Range, asked if she'd be interested in the management training program, and encouraged her to sign up. "She asked me, why wasn't I in management?" Earwood recalls. "I said, 'I'd like to talk to you about that.'" Not long afterward the two women had a follow-up conversation in which, Earwood says, Range told her she would have to move in order to be promoted, and that there were positions open in New York, Illinois, and Michigan. "She almost trie[d] to dissuade me," says Earwood, by saying, "'You know you're going to have to move. How are you going to do that?' Knowing I'm a single mother."

In fact, Earwood told Range she'd be very interested in moving to New York. "I said to her, 'Well, I like New York. That's someplace I could live.' . . . And I got real serious about it." Range told her to call her at the office to discuss it further. Earwood was excited, and told many of her coworkers she might be leaving soon to train in New York.

Earwood called Range repeatedly to follow up and left messages with her assistant, but the district manager never returned her calls.

In recent years, Wal-Mart's relocation requirement has become more ambiguous. On paper, readiness to move one's place of residence gradually disappeared as an absolute requirement for promotion. But in this lawsuit, numerous regional, district, and store-level managers have testified that in practice, this requirement was never abolished. In fact, some store managers had no idea the policy had been changed. In June 2002, Kevin Harper, the vice president of the People Division, observed under questioning from *Dukes* lawyers that regional personnel managers needed to be reminded that relocation was no longer required for employees who wanted to be promoted.

Bielby, the gender discrimination expert, noted that a "lack of clarity" and "mixed messages" on this issue could discourage women from trying to be promoted, and testimony from women confirms that it did. As Christine Kwapnoski notes, the relocation requirement was arbitrarily enforced. Where she was told that to be promoted she had to be willing to move, she saw that men were promoted within their own stores. Even if she were free to move, she says, she'd refuse on "principle, because the guys don't have to move." Earwood felt the same way. She saw numerous men promoted who were allowed to remain in their home stores. "What became an issue over the years. . . is, why do I have to relocate if this guy, this guy, this guy, this guy didn't have to relocate?" Earwood testified in her deposition, "I was surrounded by [Wal-Mart] stores within driving distance of me. Why did I have to uproot my family in order to get that promotion? It was not necessary." It seems possible that forcing employees to relocate is a tactic of labor control for Wal-Mart; it forces workers, if they are to advance in the company, to make a decision to prioritize the company over everything else in their lives. This may in fact be an effective business practice, but there's little doubt that it's unfair to women.

In the late 1980s, Wal-Mart created the Resident Assistant Manager Program, which Sam Walton was very enthusiastic about. The goal of this program was to allow people to become assistant managers and, in some cases, move into a comanager position without relocating. Testimony from Wal-Mart officials on whether this program was still in operation was vague and conflicting. Wal-Mart's executive vice president, Jim Haworth, thought the program had been phased out. Kevin Harper, the People Division VP, said it drew little participation and existed only on an "as requested" basis. Lower-level managers said they were "vaguely" aware of the program, and some had only recently learned of it—after *Dukes* was filed. Most damningly, CEO Tom Coughlin said he believed the Resident Assistant Manager Program was a dead end, and that he didn't know of a single employee who had successfully used it to advance in the company.

When the company's highest-level managers have attitudes like this, it shouldn't be surprising that even after Sam Walton's feminist epiphany, practice didn't change until the lawsuit was filed. Before 2003, even promotions into entry-level management positions (assistant manager and management trainee) have required that the employee change stores more than 60 percent of the time. These moves did not always mean that she had to move her family or find a new home—there are thousands of Wal-Mart stores, so a position nearby might be available—but they often did. To advance beyond entry level, she would most likely be required to change stores again. To become a store manager, nearly 70 percent of employees must change district, and more than a third must move to another region of the country altogether.

Of course, as Betty Dukes points out, given the company's intense centralization, Wal-Mart executives get to stay in Bentonville, where company headquarters are. They are not granting workers the kind of family stability that they themselves have—and probably value. "Maybe they'd rather not leave Bentonville!" she says. "They're raising their kids from preschool, kindergarten on to the neighborhood college, hardly ever leaving the city limits! . . . So they have to be considerate not to disrupt everyone else's life."

In his report for the plaintiffs, Bielby notes that a substantial body of social science shows that when personnel decisions are made arbitrarily or informally, they tend to be unduly influenced by stereotypes. Thus employers will assume that women are less available than men because of family commitments, or that women would rather sell baby clothes than auto parts.

Bielby found that there were many features of Wal-Mart's personnel system that were "subjective and discretionary." Only minimal written criteria were provided for promoting hourly workers into management positions. Managers were allowed to add their own criteria and to disregard them as they pleased, and there was little oversight of managers' promotion decisions. In the absence of clear guidelines, the standards were whatever managers said they were.

Bielby's findings ring true to Cleo Page, who bemusedly recalls that when she asked what she needed to do to be promoted, one store manager told her she should wear shirts with collars. "So I went and cleaned my closet and got the collared shirts," she recalls, "and dressed a little bit more higher than what I was wearing." From wearing jeans, Page moved into loafers and slacks. "It didn't work," she says and laughs ruefully, shaking her head. Whim and favoritism rather than merit shape many of Wal-Mart's personnel decisions; it is no wonder that stereotypes flourish.

One of Wal-Mart's own internal reports showed that stereotypes about women are pervasive in the company and have been a huge barrier for women seeking promotions. Many women at Wal-Mart have been told explicitly that they are not being promoted because they are women and that "women don't belong in management." When Tamara Zambrun applied for a job as a team lead (the hourly position that is frequently considered a feeder for salaried management) in Mountain Home, Idaho, her store manager, Skip Davis, said to her, "Being a female, what makes you more qualified for this job than a male employee?" Davis told her that her male coworkers might have trouble being supervised by a woman. "For over an hour," Zambrun testified in her class-member statement, "Mr. Davis required me to justify why he should give the promotion to a female instead of a male." Then he promoted a man instead.

Women describe an atmosphere of "hostility toward women in management." When Nancy Hom's director of operations called the Club he would ask to speak to a manager, even if she answered the phone. When Hom reminded him that she was a manager, rather than apologizing or admitting his mistake he'd ask her to have "one of the guys" return his call. A male assistant manager told her that the region was operated as "a good old boys club" and that he "wasn't complaining." Male managers hung out together and excluded female managers.

Working in a Cullman, Alabama, store in the early 1990s, Tammy Hall heard a male store manager tell a male assistant manager that women should be "at home with a bun in the oven" or "barefoot and pregnant." Many managers also believe that women who *are* pregnant or have children shouldn't be in management. The jewelry department head in Ohio says her manager, not wanting to promote her, constantly cited her family obligations. "It was always something. He said, 'I don't think you should go into management because you have small children.' I was like, 'don't make any decisions for me.'" Similarly, when Earwood was the personnel manager (an hourly position) in Urbana, Ohio, her store manager, Jim Phelps, asked her to add a curious stipulation to the support manager's job description. Since the support manager had to work evenings and weekends, he said, "It can't be anybody who has kids." Earwood, a single mother who had worked as a Wal-Mart support manager when her daughter was three years old, took offense.

Melissa Howard, the Bluffton, Indiana, store manager who had had to attend business meetings in the dignified environs of Hooters, was running a new Supercenter set to make a profit in its first year. In May, however, Kevin Washburn, the district manager who had invited Howard to step out for a threesome with an exotic dancer, was replaced by John Waters, who now asked her to step down and accept a demotion. The reason? A woman shouldn't be running a Wal-Mart store; Howard needed to be at home raising her daughter. Waters seemed to want to send a discouraging message to other women at the store, Howard observed in her class-member statement.

> He instructed me to step down "voluntarily" and to tell my employees at the morning meeting that having this new Supercenter was too stressful for a single parent and that I just needed to take a break. In other words, it was not enough for Mr. Waters to just get rid of me. I believe that he also wanted me to send a strong signal to other women that the job was not right for any mother. He told me to step down voluntarily, or he would have me out within four to six weeks—he would make my life "hell." I had no choice but to step down.

Another obstacle to women's advancement at Wal-Mart is the persistent segregation of departments. More than 90 percent of workers selling clothing at Wal-Mart are women, whereas less than 33 percent of those selling hardware or sporting goods are women. The gendered nature of different areas of the store is amusingly underscored by terminology like "hardlines" and "softlines." "Softlines" are clothing; "hardlines" are hardware, electronics, and other manly objects. Employees see the male-dominated departments as better stepping stones for promotion, but it's not clear that they are good stepping stones for women. According to Brad Seligman, they still don't have enough data to know. "Male" departments may just look like better routes to promotion because they have more men in them, and men are more likely than women to be promoted at Wal-Mart.

Aside from the stepping-stone issue, however, the departmental segregation often prevents women from getting experience that is often required for advancement. Dukes had been told that more floor experience was a prerequisite for promotion, but when she sought to gain additional experience she was denied the opportunity to work in "male" departments like hardware, despite having worked in hardware stores before she came to Wal-Mart. "I can mix a can of paint," she told reporters just after filing the suit in June 2001. "I want the chance to do it."[6] She shakes her head, still exasperated. "You don't have to have a man in those areas, by no means!"

And, as many plaintiffs have pointed out, segregation has a demoralizing, discouraging effect on women, sending the message that they are second-rate. Cleo Page was told by her manager that she needed to manage a bigger department before she could qualify for management training, and she hoped to manage the sporting goods department. But the manager discouraged her from applying, saying that "a man would feel more comfortable" buying sporting goods from a man. "She made it known in a store meeting not to apply if you are not a guy," says Page. "She didn't want a woman in there." That's when "I felt like I was just not going to make it."

Segregation of departments lets women know that they are not valued as much as men, and creates an environment that discourages them from seeking further promotions. In such a climate, says Dukes, "You are not going to run up to your district manager telling him you want to be promoted. You just don't have that zest and confidence." Sheila Hall asked repeatedly for a job in the hardware department of the Conway, Arkansas, store, and she finally got it when she pointed out that she'd already have it if she had "a penis between her legs"—yet as the only woman in the department she was taunted constantly by her coworkers and supervisors, who insisted that hardware was a "man's job." She eventually quit, feeling that in this environment she would never be promoted.

As Bielby points out, segregation reinforces gender stereotypes, and stereotypes create barriers to women's advancement, not just because of men's attitudes but also because they affect women's ambitions: "A large body of industrial sociology dating back to the 1950s shows that individuals who find their aspirations blocked respond by lowering their goals and aspirations."

Wal-Mart's own 1996 "Women in Leadership" report found that there was a persistent suspicion of "aggressive" women at the company. Since in any corporation, women, like men, must be aggressive to succeed, this attitude presents another significant barrier to advancement. Christine Kwapnoski says that her managers have called her "overbearing," to which her rejoinder is: "I am straightforward. I don't have time to beat around the bush. I've got a business to run. If I need something done, I'm gonna tell you it needs to get done. I'm not gonna go around going, 'Kinda sunny outside. You know, sometime today we might need to put some pallets of merchandise away.' I don't have time for that. You know, it's like, 'We need to throw a load.'" A man who acted as she does, she says, would be considered "extremely assertive. I become a 'bitch,' and I've been called that plenty of times. To my face and behind my back." On her evaluations, supervisors have characterized her as having a "tendency to intimidate others." ("I've had some interesting things written about me," she says of her evaluations. "I was moody when I was pregnant, too. Find me a pregnant woman who isn't moody! You've got something kicking you in the ribs.")

Kwapnoski, who is petite and pretty, is puzzled by her reputation. "As you can tell I'm a very intimidating person," she jokes. "Big, burly, scary." Hom, who worked in the same Sam's Club and testified that male managers deprived Kwapnoski of promotions she deserved, commented, "Christine needs to learn how to say 'Fuck you,' but smile as she says it." Kwapnoski agrees, but thinks she's only "intimidating" because she's not intimidated. "I think what intimidates the managers I've had is that I don't just take stuff, you know? You back me in a corner, yell at me, I'm not gonna start crying."

Dee Gunter, too, found that her male coworkers were put off by her competence and her assertive, confident manner. "The fact that I could take over their jobs at any time threatened them," she says and adds jokingly, "and, I'm shy!" She quickly became so knowledgeable about the tire shop—a sweaty, macho place—that customers would eagerly request her. "People would say, 'We need to speak with Dee to get this or that done,'" she recalls. "And that seemed to intimidate the men."

Sometimes women support their female coworkers' efforts to be promoted, as Nancy Hom did for Christine Kwapnoski, or provide encouragement in a sexist atmosphere, as Edith Arana did for her coworkers. But for some women, discussions with female coworkers simply confirm the hopelessness of trying to advance at Wal-Mart. After learning about how other women are treated, many conclude that the men of Wal-Mart are unlikely to give them a chance. When a female manager she admired was fired for a trivial reason, Cleo Page despaired of her own chances of advancing at Wal-Mart: "If they could fire her, after she'd been there for so long, I thought, 'Wow, I'm really expendable.'"

Even worse, some female managers deliberately sabotage the ambitions of female hourly workers. Sandra Berkowitz, a customer service representative in Boca Raton, Florida, who was supporting two grandchildren on $7.46 per hour, was explicitly discouraged from applying for an assistant-manager position. "Why bother," Ilene Jacobs, an assistant manager, told her. "Most assistant-manager jobs are held by men—unless you're an exceptional woman."

For her part, Kwapnoski knows she's an exceptionally hard worker and, despite her good-natured sense of humor, is angry that her promotion took so long. She was allowed to skip weeks of her training because it was clear to the instructor that, whereas many men in the program were new to the company, Kwapnoski was so knowledgeable about Sam's Club that there was little to teach her: "She said, 'You really have been around.'" Kwapnoski is amused by the effect *Dukes* has had on her Sam's Club career, remarking dryly, "I have a very intricate promotion timeline. It just depends what the lawsuit is doing." If the case keeps going, she jokes, she'll be running the district by the end of 2005.

Kwapnoski never saw herself as a crusader for women's rights. But the lawsuit has emboldened her to challenge her male coworkers' attitudes in her own way. She gave them a surprise at the store's last Christmas party. "I came dressed up in a short skirt, nice fancy top, makeup, hair done, high heels," she recalls. "People didn't even recognize me. They had to take double takes. 'Coach Chris, is that you?' I'm not a big makeup wearer, even if I go out," she explains, scoffing, as if it's a big joke, "I'm just a natural beauty!" She did it "so I could mess with the psyches of the men that I work with. And it worked."

Of course the stunt was a playful reference to her supervisor's absurd suggestion that she'd have a better chance of being promoted if she would "doll up," despite the fact that she was at the time working on a dirty receiving dock, sweating and unloading trucks. Interviewed nine months after the party, she says, "People still are talking about what I wore to the Christmas party. In fact somebody mentioned it today. 'I heard about what you wore. Remember that black skirt?' Oh yes, I remember. I just had to show them I could doll up, if I needed to. And boy did it make an impact." Asked if they got the reference—and the message—Kwapnoski laughs. "Oh, yes, I think they got the point. . . . I'm just full of subtleties. Part of my reputation. I think it couldn't have gotten any blunter."

Even while employed as a full-time hourly worker at Sam's Club, for most of her Wal-Mart career Kwapnoski has simultaneously held at least one other job (most recently at Toys R Us). On her Sam's Club wages alone she would have been unable to pay her Bay Area rent. Listening to her describe her work schedule in a deposition in June 5, 2002, Wal-Mart's defense lawyer, Michael Gray, was stunned: "And I thought I worked hard."

Now, as an assistant manager, Kwapnoski is finally able to get by on her Sam's Club earnings and has been able to quit her other jobs. "I don't know what to do with my free time now! I have read all of Harry Potter and two other books just since the beginning of August. I've worked the last nine years just to pay bills. I'm enjoying my free time. For now. . . but I need more books!" For the first time she's able to think more about her future happiness beyond work. "Maybe I'd like to get married again. We'll see what happens."

The dramatic improvement in Kwapnoski's life after she was promoted to assistant manager is not surprising—in fact, it is typical. By not promoting women, Wal-Mart is not only showing an indifference to hard work dramatically at odds with the company's patriotic bootstrap rhetoric, it is also trapping them in overwork and poverty.

4

ALWAYS LOW WAGES!

"I HATE INJUSTICE," says Kathleen MacDonald, a 47-year-old widow. Just five feet tall, with snow-white hair, she's not afraid to speak out, even to a representative of the U.S. military. Recently an Army recruiter called and wanted to speak to her grown son. MacDonald, who did not support the invasion of Iraq, gave him a piece of her mind. "Why don't you call some of these rich children?" she demanded. He hasn't called back since.

MacDonald has worked as a sales clerk and stocker for 14 years in a Wal-Mart in Aiken, South Carolina (Strom Thurmond's birthplace), not far from the Georgia border. She was a cashier and clerk at Kroger, a grocery chain, for a couple of years before coming to Wal-Mart. MacDonald has worked in Wal-Mart's toys, housewares, pets, lawn and garden, and stationery departments, and now the candy department. She likes her work at the Aiken store and has no ambition to become a manager. "I don't need the stress," she says good-naturedly.

Yet MacDonald says, "When I do a job, I take pride in doing it." She consistently earns excellent evaluations, and she likes keeping her department neat. Most of all, she says, "I like talking to people." She was pleased with the training the company provided: "You were very well trained in the mechanics of keeping the merchandise on the shelf straight and clean and priced." But she's seen more than a few injustices in the store, and Wal-Mart, like the Army recruiter, has been finding out just how she feels.

"At my store, male associates brag about their pay," she testified in her *Dukes* class-member statement. After listening to enough of them brag, MacDonald began to realize that if they were telling the truth about their wages, she was being paid less than men who were doing the very same job, even though she'd been with the company longer. When she complained about this, the meat department manager told her that males stocking groceries make more money than females stocking "female" items because "stocking cans was harder than stocking clothes." Another supervisor told her that women would never be paid more than men because they "don't physically stack up."

MacDonald was no stranger to Bible Belt sexism. Having grown up in a Catholic family in Chelsea, Massachusetts, a working-class city on the other side of the Mystic River from Boston, she moved down to South Carolina with her husband and her mother in the early 1980s. Her mother had grown tired of the cold weather in New England, and her husband thought a small town might be a better place to raise children than Chelsea.

"I'm not gonna lie about it," she says, "I'm a Yankee, a liberal." She confesses to some culture shock living in a small town down South: "Everything is a sin here. We cannot sell general merchandise till one-thirty on Sunday. You can't sell alcoholic beverages after midnight on Saturdays or Sundays. No gambling."

But of all cultural peculiarities, it is gender relations in the region that MacDonald has found most troubling, and she still isn't used to its old-fashioned hierarchies. She was not raised to be subordinate to men. "My mother ruled the roost," she says proudly. The only girl, with four brothers, MacDonald played baseball, and her brothers were taught to do chores. "My mother taught my brothers just like she taught me: how to cook, how to wash clothes, how to wash dishes," MacDonald says. "There was no discrimination whatsoever, just because they were boys. . . . And I'll tell you that if you ask their wives, they'll tell you that it was the best thing she could have ever done. And my father never told my mother how to think, how to act, what her opinion was." MacDonald says she has tried to instill similar ideals in her kids, two daughters and a son, now in their twenties. Her own marriage was egalitarian, like that of her parents: "My husband never told me how I should vote, what I should believe," she says. "He understood that I was my own person."

With that kind of attitude, MacDonald stands out in Aiken—and at Wal-Mart. "Women here won't speak up for themselves," she laments in the heavy Boston accent she still has after 20 years in the South, and notes that women she knows in Aiken even let their husbands tell them how to vote. "If their husbands believe one way, they are expected to believe the same way." Still, nothing could have prepared MacDonald for the extraordinary explanation her department manager, Joel Batson, provided for the different pay rates between men and women in the store. Women, he told her, "will never make as much money as men." Surprised, MacDonald asked why. Batson explained, "God made Adam first, so women will always be second to men." Years later, MacDonald was still incredulous. "This is what he tells me! Isn't it incredible that you could believe this crap?" She adds, "He agreed some men take it to the extreme—when they beat their women."

Awful as MacDonald's story seems, the data, according to experts hired by the *Dukes* plaintiffs, tells an even worse tale. In February 2003, Richard Drogin, the expert statistician hired by the plaintiffs, examined promotion and pay patterns in most of Wal-Mart's major U.S. operations from 1996 through the first quarter of 2002. He reviewed the complete job histories of 3,945,151 workers. In 2001, the average woman working full-time at Wal-Mart earned about $5,000 less annually than the average man at the company. In every single region of the country, men made at least $2,200 more than women.[1] At Wal-Mart, Drogin concluded, women make less money than men, not only because they tend to hold lower-paying positions, but also because they earn less money than men holding the same jobs.

In the September 2003 class-certification hearing, Brad Seligman, the plaintiffs' lead counsel, stated: "It's. . . undisputed on this record, that [Wal-Mart's] female retail store employees, hourly and salaried. . . are paid less than men in every year since. . . 1996, and in every region of Wal-Mart, and that female employees on average are paid less than male employees in virtually every major job position in the retail stores."

Of all the charges that make up the *Dukes v. Wal-Mart Stores, Inc.* suit, the one that most people will find the simplest to grasp—and perhaps the most disturbing—is that women are paid less than men doing the same jobs. One can argue about whether women want to be promoted as much as men do—and much of the outcome of *Dukes* will depend on who wins that argument—but no one can doubt that they'd like to be paid just as well for doing exactly the same work. Cashiers are the lowest-paid workers at Wal-Mart, and 92.6 percent of them are women.[2] Yet even the company's (few) male cashiers make more money than their female counterparts: $14,525, as compared to $13,831.[3]

Female hourly workers at Wal-Mart earned about $1,100 less per year than male hourly workers. Women's total lower earnings are partly explained by their working fewer hours, as many more women than men do work part-time. But that's not the whole story. Women's hourly rates were, on average, 30 cents per hour lower than those of men. The average national wage for male cashiers at the company, $8.33 per hour, is higher than that for women, $8.05.

Female managers, all of whom must work full-time, aren't living on poverty wages, but they still are subjected to pay discrimination, as Stephanie Odle learned from that fateful peek at her coworker's tax form. Drogin found that the over-all difference between all male and all female managers' compensation is about $14,500, and some disparity was found at every level of management. A male assistant manager makes on average $39,790, whereas a woman doing the same job makes on average $37,322.

Numerous testimonies from women support Drogin's data. Micki Earwood, one of the original *Dukes* plaintiffs, was overjoyed when she finally landed a job as a personnel manager in the Urbana, Ohio, Wal-Mart. An outgoing and sympathetic "people person," she had coveted the position for years, knowing she would be good at it. "Anybody who was my friend in that store knew how badly I wanted that job," she recalls. Sadly, she now says, the personnel job taught her how badly women at Wal-Mart were treated, for she saw all her coworkers' files and observed that men were paid better than women who worked in exactly the same positions. "I was trusted with a lot of information," she says, "and the problem is that the more you know, the more disgusted you get at the company, if you're someone who doesn't put blinders on or isn't brainwashed."

She bore no personal ill will toward her male coworkers—in fact, they were her friends. "I really got along with these gentlemen who made better money," she says, "and you know, they discussed it with me. They knew what I made, and they'd joke about it. I'd say, 'Hey, I don't begrudge you making good money. I just think the rest of us ought to be making what you're making.'" Once she was proud to work at Wal-Mart, but now says, "If I wasn't part of this lawsuit, I'd never tell anybody that I worked there. I'm ashamed that I worked for a company that treated people that way."

As a woman advances upward in Wal-Mart's hierarchy, she actually faces ever more dramatic pay disparities with her male counterparts. The higher the management job, the greater the gap in percentage terms. It is relatively small between male and female management trainees, the gateway to the assistant-manager position, which is Wal-Mart's entry-level management job. But it becomes ever more marked at the store-manager level, where males earn $105,682 and women 16 percent less ($89,280); even more so at the district-manager level ($239,519 to $177,149), and downright staggering for regional vice presidents ($419,435 to $279,772, a difference of 33 percent).

"I had the title but not the pay," says Gretchen Adams, who, as a comanager (second-in-command to the store manager), opened 27 Supercenters. "They take us for idiots." Adams worked for the company for eight years, supporting her son and her disabled husband, and relocated her family eight times at Wal-Mart's request. Blonde and athletic, Adams gives an impression of physical strength and formidable competence. At Wal-Mart, she trained men with little to no relevant experience, who then earned starting salaries of $3,500 a year more than her own. Working as a comanager in Las Vegas, she learned that two of her fellow comanagers, who had no more experience than she, earned about $47,000 each, while she made $43,500. When she complained, she got a raise (to $47,000), but no retroactive pay, and no explanation. What made her especially angry was that she asked the company to conduct a review to see if other women were also being underpaid and received no assurance that such a study would take place; indeed, as far as she knows, it never did.

The gap also widens the longer a female hourly worker stays at Wal-Mart. According to Drogin's report, female hourly workers start behind male hourly workers who start at the company at the same time, and they fall progressively further behind. A female hourly worker is paid 35 cents less per hour than a man hired to do the same job. And after five years at Wal-Mart, that man makes $1.16 per hour more than she does. "That's what happens in the store," says Betty Dukes. "You and I have the same hire date, but you're living and I'm barely existing."

Many women are paid less than men who are newer to the company. "It just makes you sick," Earwood says now. "I would see a two-year associate who was a male bike assembler, and he was making more than a female department manager who'd been there eight or nine years. There was no way they could justify that to me." Christine Kwapnoski, the *Dukes* plaintiff who is now an assistant manager in Concord, California, was consistently paid less than men who hadn't been in their jobs as long, and despite a stellar performance, she often did not get merit raises that were given to men. A frequent Sam's Club Associate of the Month, her apartment is cluttered with appreciation plaques for, among other things, converting Pace supermarkets in California to Sam's Clubs. This isn't unusual: the earnings gaps exist *despite women's superior performance evaluations,* and despite the fact that pay is supposed to be based partly on performance. In 2001, performance ratings of women hourly workers were higher overall than those of men, and for the major hourly positions—sales associates, cashiers, department managers—women scored higher than men doing the same jobs. In 75 percent of hourly jobs, women scored better than their male counterparts.

It's not only that women do not have pay parity with men in the same job: frequently, women earn less than men who are in positions of lesser responsibility. Melissa Howard, the Indiana store manager who was dragged to a strip club, came to Wal-Mart in 1992 with six years of Kmart experience, much of it supervisory. Hired as a Wal-Mart department manager at $6 an hour, she worked her way up and became a store manager in 1998. Running a Supercenter in Bluffton, Indiana, Howard supervised a man with no Wal-Mart experience who made $65,000 a year, $15,000 more than her own salary. Furthermore, as a new hire he was given three weeks of vacation; Howard had to work at Wal-Mart for seven years to get the same amount of vacation time. Another man Howard supervised was hired at a salary exceeding hers by $10,000.

Like Kathleen MacDonald, many women have been given startling "explanations" for the pay disparities at Wal-Mart. Ramona Scott is a single mother who worked for the company for eight years. As a personnel manager in a Wal-Mart in Pinellas Park, Florida, Scott, like Earwood, had access to her coworkers' pay information and was appalled by the wage disparities between men and women and by the fact that men were given more overtime. Scott asked her store manager to explain these differences. He said, "Men are here to make a career and women aren't. Retail is for housewives who just need to earn extra money."

Even more infuriating is the most common rationalization: Many women at Wal-Mart—many of them single mothers— have been told that a male coworker deserves to be paid more because he has "a family" to support. Joyce Moody, a former Wal-Mart manager who worked with the company for more than 20 years, most of that time in Mississippi stores or in the Home Office, says this way of thinking is firmly entrenched in company culture. "I have been told when I was hiring folks, 'He's the man of the house, start him off at this, start her off at that,'" says Moody, who is now a witness in *Dukes*. "I mean, I have been told that, and it's not fair."

Wal-Mart argues that women are paid less in part because they choose to work in departments that don't pay as well— ladies' wear as opposed to sporting goods, for example. This is merely another way of saying that what looks like discrimination is really a consequence of women's own choices. In her argument, during the September 2003 class-certification hearing, Wal-Mart's lead counsel, Nancy Abell, of the law firm Paul, Hastings, Janofsky & Walker, pointed out that Drogin's data analysis didn't differentiate by department, and instead treated hourly employees in all categories "as if everybody in them ought to be treated the same." Without analyzing for department-to-department differences, comparing pay among hourly workers is "meaningless," she said—in fact and apparently unwittingly conceding that departments were segregated, and that "male" departments paid better. She argued that Drogin should have compared employees within departments, as Wal-Mart's expert, Nancy Haworth, did. "There are different market rates for sales workers who sell different products," Abell argued. "Wal-Mart obviously has to pay according to the market." (In an astute pubic relations move, Wal-Mart hired a woman as its lead counsel, thus one-upping the plaintiffs, whose lead counsels are both men.[4]) Abell's co-counsel, Paul Grossman, argued along similar lines, citing one store manager, "Edna, in Lawrence, Kansas," who had to give her electronics employees a $2-per-hour raise when Circuit City moved next door, so they wouldn't jump ship and work for the competing retailer.

Drogin agreed that the better-paying areas of the store were predominantly male, but he viewed this segregation as part of Wal-Mart's pattern of discrimination—not, as Wal-Mart's lawyers apparently see it, as evidence that the inequality between men and women's pay is a function of natural inequalities between male and female skills and desires. Plaintiffs' argument is that the reason male-dominated departments pay better is that men favor those departments.

Just as segregation in the pre-Civil Rights movement United States sent a clear message that blacks were inferior, sex segregation in the workplace sends a profoundly demoralizing message to women, implying that their lower pay is deserved because their work isn't worth as much as men's. "It was very humiliating," says Edith Arana of her store manager's policy of segregating departments. "He didn't want certain people in certain jobs, because they were women. . . . You can have twenty-five women who are more than able to do a job and one man [who is] a cashier and just got out of high school, and [the manager] will give [the job in hardware] to him over these twenty-five women, because hardware is a 'man's job.'"

Grossman argued that Drogin's analysis made too much of seniority and evaluations, when, in fact, in determining a worker's pay, "our store managers consider hundreds of factors that aren't in that allegedly fancy computer base." This comment brings to mind the traditional phrase employed by orthodox economists to justify discrimination: pay and promotion exist because of workers' "unobserved characteristics." In other words, as Heather Boushey, an economist at the Center on Economic and Policy Research, wryly puts it: "Women and minorities are so incompetent that it makes economic sense not to promote them."

For example, Grossman continued, warming to his argument, Drogin's model neglected pre–Wal-Mart experience—"the single most important factor in setting hourly pay. . . when someone is hired." Information about employees' experience before Wal-Mart, he said, isn't in any database, and that's why experts on both sides were unable to factor it into a statistical analysis, but store managers interviewed by Wal-Mart's legal team strongly emphasized it. He argued that experienced meatcutters (nearly 80 percent of whom are male) and anyone with produce or electronics experience—areas that are predominantly male—is paid more.

Grossman may be right that differences in pre–Wal-Mart experience partly accounts for some of the pay disparity between men and women. Certainly, women are more likely than men to spend time out of the workforce raising children. They're also more likely to be working at Wal-Mart to get off welfare, or to have held low-wage, low-status jobs prior to coming to Wal-Mart. None of this is Wal-Mart's fault.

Yet many plaintiffs and witnesses complain that they were paid less than men *despite* years of relevant pre–Wal-Mart experience. Dee Gunter began work at Wal-Mart with 35 years of retail experience, including 8 years in management. "I worked in fast foods, J. C. Penney, pet shops, video stores," she recalls, "pretty much any kind of sales you can name." Indeed, many middle-aged women have testified to being paid less than teenage boys, who can't possibly have the more impressive resumes. Elizabeth Monroe, a sales associate in the electronics department in Aberdeen, North Carolina, had 16 years of experience as the owner and manager of a store. She started at $5.75 an hour, while male cart pushers who were still in high school were hired at an hourly wage of over $6.

In addition to contesting plaintiffs' data, Wal-Mart has argued that some of the *Dukes* plaintiffs aren't proper representatives of the 1.6 million-member class, and has contested their specific claims. In the September 2003 hearing, Abell argued that most of the named plaintiffs in *Dukes* were paid better than most men in their stores, so they were not the best examples of the problem "they're claiming to represent." Indeed, she pointed out, some of the *Dukes* plaintiffs were among the best-paid workers in their stores.

Some of them are. But the justice of the *Dukes* case—and the appropriateness of these particular plaintiffs to represent the class—depends not on whether they were paid better than many men in the store, but on whether they would have made more money if they'd been men. Christine Kwapnoski is one of the better-paid employees in her store—with good reason, since she has been with the company for 17 years. Yet she is paid virtually the same amount as a coworker, John Salamone, who has been with Sam's Club for half that time.

In some sense, some named plaintiffs in *Dukes* are speaking up for women who are even worse off than they are. The women at the very bottom of the Wal-Mart hierarchy, those who earn the least, are far less likely to speak out against the company's abuses.

Women who speak out tend either to have been with the company for a long time and now are making considerably more than minimum wage, or have some measure of economic security from outside Wal-Mart—sometimes a husband or boyfriend with a better job, a widow's social security, or a house whose mortgage was paid off long ago, in better times. As those I interviewed often pointed out, many of the hourly employees at Wal-Mart are single mothers who are so terrified of losing their jobs that they may never dare speak out in support of the *Dukes* plaintiffs, let alone put forth claims of their own.

There's another good reason women often don't complain about the disparities. "I've always been paid less [than men]," says Kwapnoski. "But for a great many years in my career [at Sam's Club], wages were top secret. You'd get fired if you said anything to anybody about wages."

This "gag rule" was not just a quirk of Kwapnoski's club or the Sam's Club division of the company. Until recently, Wal-Mart, like many companies, had a company-wide policy prohibiting employees from discussing their wages with anybody, inside or outside the company. In addition to being a shrewd mechanism of managerial control over all employees, this rule often keeps workers from immediately identifying the unfair wage disparities between men and women. "A lot of the reason they didn't want the salaries talked about was because there was great favoritism," says Dukes, "and there still is." Even when women do realize inequality exists, the rule keeps them from speaking out.

Though this prohibition against discussing wages used to be found on every Wal-Mart employee's annual summary of wages and benefits, it is illegal under federal and most state law. When an administrative judge in 1999 in Grand Rapids, Michigan, declared the "gag rule" illegal and ordered Wal-Mart to "cease and desist" from restricting workers' conversation about wages, the rule disappeared from traceable employee paperwork. Wal-Mart appealed that decision, but in summer 2003, the National Labor Relations Board upheld the Grand Rapids judge's ruling.[5]

However, many workers still believe the "gag rule" exists. You might expect an employee in the Home Office to be up-to-date on a four-year-old policy change, but in June 2003, Brenda Barrerra, a customer complaint hotline worker (whom I interviewed on the Bentonville town square), refused to disclose her salary because, she said, it was against company rules to do so. Chris Kwapnoski, interviewed in September 2003, says "a lot" of her coworkers still think discussing wages is against Wal-Mart rules. She says she has to keep reminding people, "'It's not taboo anymore!'" But she admits that she, too, sometimes forgets that it's now a permissible topic of discussion. Dukes was surprised to hear that the rule had changed. "It has not been promoted that it has been changed," she said.

It makes sense that workers think it is still against Wal-Mart rules to discuss wages, says Al Zack, a just-retired vice president of the United Food and Commercial Workers Union, which is trying to organize Wal-Mart workers: even though the rule is no longer stated in company literature, Wal-Mart still discourages employees from talking about their pay. As recently as 2003, some managers were still warning against such conversation in new employees' orientation. Clearly, even if forbidding employees to talk about wages is illegal and done unofficially, it is still a crucial part of Wal-Mart's strategy to keep all employees underpaid and to keep women uninformed about their unfair treatment.

In her deposition by Wal-Mart's lawyers, Arana recalled a meeting with her store manager in which she asked for a raise: "I just told him I was working my butt off, and that my feet hurt just like his feet hurt, and the only difference is I still have to go home and take care of another family [other than the "Wal-Mart family"]. I told him, 'I want this raise and you know I deserve it.'" That time, her hourly wage went up from $9.44 to $10 per hour.

At Wal-Mart, as at many companies, merit raises are supposed to be tied to performance ratings. A "standard" rating on an evaluation indicates average work, as opposed to an "exceeds expectations" rating, which is above average. If someone tried to give Arana a standard evaluation, she would complain. "I told them, I don't do 'standard' work. They would come to me with that... *bullcrap*"—a religious and reserved woman, she pauses, trying to decide whether it's okay to use this word—"and I'd go, 'Uh-uh. Got another piece of paper?'" As a result of her assertiveness, her evaluations were outstanding, and her merit raises consistently high. Debra Smith of Equal Rights Advocates (ERA), one of Arana's lawyers, explains that in the deposition, Wal-Mart's lawyers used Arana's merit raises against her. They said, "'You've got more raises than anybody we know! How can you say you were discriminated against? Look, you got a dollar raise.' The only reason she got it is she would point out, 'Look, I deserve more than a 25-cent raise.' And she'd get [a better one].... She wasn't confrontational," says Smith, "but she knew her worth. During her evaluation she would say, 'I really deserve a raise.' Most people would get these 25-cent raises, but she stood up for herself."

Arana's experience in succeeding in getting merit raises—especially given that she was being discriminated against in promotions—points out another potential explanation for the pay disparity among men and women at Wal-Mart besides outright discrimination. Given Wal-Mart is a notoriously stingy employer—and not unionized—employees who are not aggressive in negotiations are at a profound disadvantage. Research indicates that women are less assertive than men in many different kinds of negotiations, including those with employers, and that this works profoundly to their disadvantage. Exceptions such as Arana merely highlight the rule.

"You can't be quiet with Wal-Mart," says Dedra ("Dee") Farmer, a former manager from Lawrence, Kansas, who was recently fired from the company after 13 years' service, possibly, she thinks, in retaliation for being a witness in the *Dukes* case. "You can't sit and pat yourself on the back. You need to ask for merit raises all the time." Obviously, it's cheaper for Wal-Mart to give raises only to those who make the most noise. But such practices clearly favor men—and in any case, being a skilled and persistent negotiator shouldn't be a precondition for a living wage in a retail job.

Furthermore, at many Wal-Mart stores, managers are so abusive to the women who work under them that reasoned negotiation simply isn't possible. Micki Earwood recalls incidents she witnessed as a personnel manager in Urbana, Ohio. When women asked the store manager for raises, "He would make them beg. They would say, 'Jeez, I'm only making X amount of money, and I think I deserve a merit raise. I'm running a top department, I'm number one in the district,' and he'd say to them, 'Well, why do you think you should get more money? Why do you think you should get it as opposed to anyone else who's doing well. . . . He would make them have to explain and explain." He never did that to men. In fact, some men were routinely awarded merit raises without even having to ask for them.

As Dukes points out, men are more likely to ask for raises at Wal-Mart because they are friendly with the managers. Asking for more money is awkward, but far less so when you know that you are liked and respected. A woman is "not going to ask for a merit raise because there is nothing personable that would make you feel comfortable. . . . There is always a [feeling of] rejection when you ask for something and don't get it. . . . You think, 'What's wrong, am I not good enough? How come I'm not getting it?'" To ask for a raise at all, "You have to feel as though they are really hot about you."

Many women at Wal-Mart are unlikely to feel that management is "hot" about them, since they are constantly being insulted and told how inferior they are. When Gretchen Adams was a comanager in Las Vegas, her district manager called her a "worthless broad." Sheila Hall, the hardware worker in Conway, Arkansas, was told that that she might get paid more if she wore lower-cut shirts. But even worse, when she told her store manager that competitors were paying better, he said, "The way I see it, a whore for a quarter is a whore for a quarter."

Even without such extreme and explicit verbal insults, many women at Wal-Mart feel their pay stubs convey the same devastating message: they and their hard work are not valued. A few years ago, Dukes's store manager conducted a salary review, and called her into his office to announce that he was raising her per-hour wage. Dukes was hopeful, thinking that maybe her life was about to get a lot easier. "I've been trying to get a salary increase in this store for months," he told her. The "increase" was only ten cents an hour. "It was a total insult, a big old spin," Dukes recalls, still smarting from the incident. "He felt he was doing something for me, and shook my hand and signed the wage increase. I kept my cool. My mother always said you have to keep your cool—you can't yell and fuss. But it was degrading, to say the least. A dime." At the time there was no way for her to express the depth of the injury. "I can't just walk off the job and say, I'm so insulted, I just cannot rise," she say with a gesture of mock melodrama. "I clocked in on time the next morning, because I still needed my job. And [the Wal-Mart managers] knew it. That was an ugly thing to do, to give an associate a ten-cent raise."

For many women, these humiliations are compounded by having to rely on the goodwill of the community for their very survival. Some women at Wal-Mart must depend on charity to get by, as many good-hearted Americans learn every holiday season. Several years ago, Philip Kellerman, who is active in charitable efforts in upstate New York, took a family holiday shopping at an Oneonta, New York, Wal-Mart as part of his Rotary Club's effort to help families too poor to buy gifts for their children. He was surprised and deeply saddened to learn that the mother of the family worked in that very same Wal-Mart.[6] Her wages were so meager that even with her employee discount, Wal-Mart's "low, low prices" still weren't low enough for her to do her Christmas shopping.

Fellow Wal-Mart workers would not be so surprised. When they worked at Wal-Mart, Dee Farmer and Alix McKenna (also a former Wal-Mart employee), a lesbian couple who have raised three children together, tried to look after their fellow associates, and to speak out against discrimination and low wages. "It's like protecting your young," says McKenna. "I always say, every store manager should be a mother." The two say that in the Lawrence, Kansas, Wal-Mart store where they worked, every year employees choose a "Christmas family," a needy family in the community, and donate their own money to make their holiday season a brighter one. For five years in a row, the associates have chosen a female worker in their own store.

"Raina," a cashier whose family has been chosen twice, has three children. "And of course her husband doesn't pay any child support," says Farmer, "so she's living on a Wal-Mart check." Raina got cancer and, as Farmer observes, "Once you fall behind [on your bills], it's really easy to keep falling behind." Another woman who was chosen had three children, one of them a new baby, and a boyfriend in jail. A third woman had three girls "and she was working two jobs to try to make things meet. And still couldn't, so [hers] was a Christmas family too." A fourth woman was living in a camper with her two children and her teenage daughter's baby. According to McKenna, employees are dismayed when they realize that their coworkers are so needy: "People do feel that it's wrong. They realize, 'Oh my God, this person works right beside me and they were the Christmas family, obviously because Wal-Mart's not paying them enough.'"

Many more Wal-Mart employees rely on public assistance for their survival, including Food Stamps, for which the income cutoff is low: 130 percent of the federal poverty line. Poverty is defined by the government as an annual income of $14,810 per year for a family of three. Many Wal-Mart workers also depend on Medicaid; since Wal-Mart makes its employees pay for one third of their health insurance premiums, only 50 percent choose to be covered by the company plan.

"The insurance is just a joke," says April Hotchkiss, a striking 22-year-old sales clerk with blond streaks in her long, curly brown hair who works full-time in a Pueblo, Colorado, Wal-Mart. Last September, she went to the hospital with an ulcer. "Wal-Mart paid for everything—except for two thousand dollars of it. When you are barely making nine hundred a month, that is a lot of money." The official at the hospital looked at Hotchkiss's pay stubs and was appalled— "She was like, 'holy crap'"—and immediately agreed that she qualified for the Colorado Indigent Care Program. "So I only had to pay twenty dollars because I am so low income." An assistant manager at her store who was new to Wal-Mart was shocked to hear this story. "He about crapped his pants," says Hotchkiss. "I told him, 'Don't worry, the taxpayers are going to pay for it. Just know that this is who you sold your soul to.'"

"Isn't that terrible?" asks Gretchen Adams, the former Wal-Mart manager, of the fact that the company's full-time workers must depend on public assistance. Adams was deeply ashamed that many of the women working under her were forced to collect Food Stamps and other forms of welfare. Wal-Mart's reliance on the already thin social safety net has become a political issue in California, and stands to become a national issue as well, one particularly dramatized by the pay inequalities and inadequacies exposed by *Dukes v. Wal-Mart Stores, Inc.* Taxpayers are subsidizing Wal-Mart, and responsible government officials are getting worried. In February 2004, the office of the Democratic congressman George Miller released a report showing that each Wal-Mart store employing 200 people costs taxpayers $420,750 per year in public assistance.[7] One state tax official in the Midwest, characterizing Wal-Mart's "benefit package" as "Food Stamps and Medicaid," says, "I can't believe towns around here think a new Wal-Mart represents economic development."[8]

In one of many extremely misleading commercials that portrays Wal-Mart as a great place to work, a young father speaks movingly of his baby, who was born with a liver disease. The child would not have survived, we're led to believe, without Wal-Mart's tender care and generosity. In reality, workers at Wal-Mart must pay out of their wages, which average $8 an hour, between 41 and 47 percent of the cost of the company's health plan. This is particularly disgraceful in light of the fact that big corporations tend to offer overwhelmingly better health insurance than small businesses, and Wal-Mart is the biggest company of all. If the young father had worked for another large company, he likely would have paid just 25 percent of the cost of health coverage for his family.

Who would fault Wal-Mart for covering the treatment of a baby's serious liver disease? Still, the company health plan is heavily weighted toward such catastrophic illnesses, and not toward the preventive care that many more children need. That baby, though he or she survived liver cancer, is likely still missing out on many of the medical advances that dramatically improved children's health in the twentieth-century, such as immunization for measles, mumps, or rubella—vaccinations all strongly recommended by the American Academy of Pediatrics but not covered by Wal-Mart's plan.[9] And if that young father were new to Wal-Mart, even as a full-time worker he'd have to wait six months for the health plan to cover his family. If he worked for another large retailer, he and his family would likely be covered after 1.3 to 2.5 months.[10]

A recent state study found that the children of Wal-Mart workers in Georgia were enrolled in Peachcare, the state's program for needy children, at a rate higher than that of any other company—indeed, the rate was 14 times that of the private employer with the next-highest rate of dependency on the program.[11] More than 10,000 children of Wal-Mart workers were enrolled in the program. The study found one Wal-Mart child in the program for every four of the company's Georgia employees. Studies of other states, including Washington State,[12] have also found that Wal-Mart had more employees (and their family members) crowding the welfare rolls than any other company.

It is ironic that in the post-Clinton era, when most welfare for the poor is short term—individuals can generally now depend on it for only a few years—Wal-Mart, the richest company in the world, can benefit from welfare indefinitely and never be thrown off. Time limits for poor families are now enforced rigorously, and conservative politicians at both the state and federal level are trying to change the laws in order to shove people off welfare even more quickly. But there is no cap on how long a corporation like Wal-Mart can benefit from welfare's supplement to workers, no deadline after which an employer must begin paying a living wage and decent benefits. Equally outrageous is the fact that Wal-Mart benefits from a more traditional source of public funding, from towns that can't afford such outflows, who pay Wal-Mart millions of dollars, in both tax credits and cash give-aways, so that the retailer will set up shop and further drain their resources by underpaying women. It is curious that Wal-Mart—the icon of American free enterprise and self-sufficiency, founded by a man who is revered as a truly "self-made success—turns out to be one of the biggest "welfare queens" of our time.

Wal-Mart is a low-wage employer, and would be a drain on public coffers even without discrimination. But it is clear that discrimination adds significantly to the problem. The public costs of women's inequality have been well documented. Eliminating sex discrimination would raise most family incomes, except in the minority of households where the woman doesn't work at all outside the home. Taxpayers could rejoice, too: a recent study found that nearly 40 percent of poor working women receiving public assistance could leave the welfare rolls if they were to receive "pay equity increases," wage hikes to bring their earnings in line with those of male coworkers.[13] Considering the impact Wal-Mart already has on the American economy, it is fair to say that correcting pay inequity at Wal-Mart would have a significant effect on the lives of millions of people, men as well as women.

It is curious that equal pay isn't seen as a hot-button issue by the media or the political establishment (like, say, gay rights or abortion), because most women care about it—a lot. In June 2003, the Center for the Advancement of Women (CAW), a research organization founded by Faye Wattleton, the former head of Planned Parenthood, released a two-year study of attitudes toward feminism. When more than 3,300 American women were asked what the priorities of the organized women's rights movement should be, 90 percent cited "equal pay for equal work" as a top concern—many more than those who cited abortion rights, which scored just 41 percent.[14] Asked to pick which issue was most important to them personally, "equal pay for equal work" was "by far the most popular choice," reported the researchers.

Forty-three percent of the respondents in CAW's survey said that they, personally, had experienced sex discrimination, which is not surprising since pay discrimination remains a persistent problem for women in every industry.[15] In 2002, women were paid 76 cents for every dollar men received. This problem has the potential to politically unite women in nearly every job category: female physicians earn 58.3 percent of their male colleagues' salaries; although 95 percent of nurses are women, male nurses make 9 percent more than their female counterparts; female college professors' earnings are 78.6 percent of male professors'; waitresses make 87.2 percent of what waiters make.[16]

Pay discrimination has been illegal since the passage of the 1964 Civil Rights Act, which includes a provision called Title VII, the law under which the *Dukes* plaintiffs are suing Wal-Mart. Title VII prohibits paying women less than men, even if their jobs are different—if the reason for the pay gap is the workers' sex.

The CAW survey revealed that many women who were concerned about equal pay didn't think of themselves as feminists: only 9 percent of the respondents regarded "feminist" as a "completely positive" term, and 31 percent saw it as "negative." Across demographic groups, regardless of religion or political affiliation, women thought "equal pay" was a "top priority." Twenty-eight percent of the women responding to the survey were Republicans, and 45 percent of the respondents were Evangelical or born-again Christians.

The *Dukes* plaintiffs are the kind of people many of these nonfeminists can identify with. Dee Gunter, a 54-year-old conservative Republican, is fairly typical of many of the women in the CAW survey and in the United States generally. She does not call herself a feminist. Like four out of the six current *Dukes* plaintiffs, she is a fundamentalist Christian who does not see herself as a "women's libber."

Asked why fighting discrimination at work doesn't make her a "women's libber," Gunter reveals a lot of curious notions about organized feminism. "I don't think that—for lack of a better way to put it—castrating a man ever accomplished anything. I did very well as a female before the women's lib thing. And I think it sent a negative message to men. They don't know their place in society." Yet equal pay is an absolute for Gunter, and she strongly believes it's worth fighting for.

Still, the pay issue is practically invisible in public debate. Politicians are not asked about equal pay, nor does it feature prominently on political TV shows. Even among organized feminists, equal pay and other matters of workplace equality often take a back seat to reproductive rights. That could change if *Dukes v. Wal-Mart* remains in the public eye, because Wal-Mart is such a high-profile company and is part of so many Americans' everyday lives—whether as an employer or a shopping destination—and because the *Dukes* plaintiffs are so atypical of the (still pervasive though mostly unfair) public stereotype of "women's libbers" as elite women who don't have to worry about bread-and-butter issues, whose values are somehow at odds with "families." Living paycheck to paycheck, most of them Christian and deeply dedicated to their families, the plaintiffs could draw sympathy from many who have historically been hostile to feminism.

As important as it is to expose Wal-Mart's unequal pay scale, it's also crucial to remember that Wal-Mart is a low-wage employer, and many of the hourly jobs will never be good ones, even if men and women get paid the same for doing them. Not everybody can become a store manager, and most male hourly workers, though they make more than their female coworkers, still do not earn a living wage, averaging $16,526 a year. In 2001, the average Wal-Mart worker made $8.21 per hour. "Most women at Wal-Mart are never going to make $20 an hour," says Debra Smith of ERA.

For that reason, ERA is also working to fight discrimination in the skilled trades. The group's aim is not only to improve Wal-Mart, but also to ensure that women have more employment opportunities, meaning that fewer women ever have to work there. As one employment-law scholar points out, the best possible outcome in *Dukes v. Wal-Mart* is still not an inspiring one: men and women at the company will be "equally screwed. Not to be cynical," she sighs, "but it's still not going to make things that much better."

5

POSSIBILITIES
AND LIMITATIONS

B_{ETTY} D_{UKES} $_{V.}$ $W_{AL-}M_{ART}$ S_{TORES} is the largest sex discrimination class-action suit ever filed against a private employer and, indeed, the scale and scope of Wal-Mart's female troubles are extreme. Yet sex discrimination is a problem throughout the retail industry, the sector upon which poor women increasingly depend for employment. While the retail industry average of 40 to 50 percent female management is better than Wal-Mart's 33 percent, it's still not great, considering that most of the sector's hourly workers are women. Clearly the retail industry suffers from a systemic problem, of which Wal-Mart is just a particularly egregious example.

In his autobiography Sam Walton wrote:

In the old days [retailers] didn't think women could handle anything but the clerk jobs because the managers usually did so much physical labor—unloading trucks and hauling merchandise out of the stockroom. . . . Nowadays, the industry has waked up to the fact that women make great retailers. So we at Wal-Mart, along with everybody else, have to do everything we can to recruit and attract women.[1]

Walton was right that some of the industry's sexism has historically been connected with attitudes and culture. But it is also related to the powerlessness of low-wage workers: living paycheck to paycheck, women facing discrimination in these jobs frequently cannot afford to complain and risk losing them. They are usually not unionized, so they have no one to complain to when managers break the rules.

Because retailers regard the jobs as low-skill, they view workers as interchangeable. A worker in a Reno, Nevada, Wal-Mart, a single mother of four who did not want her name used, says she used to feel that Wal-Mart was missing out on her contributions by not promoting her: "They have wasted talent and knowledge by keeping me where I cannot be as effective." But lately she's been realizing that her personal potential probably doesn't matter to Wal-Mart. "Just another ant in the massive hill is all I am to them," she muses, "A dispensable ant in a vast army of workers." When workers' individual contributions are valued so little, companies have less incentive to correct discrimination and encourage meritocratic decision making.

Because promotion criteria are often vague in so-called low-skilled jobs, favoritism is rampant. One West Coast lawyer who frequently represents retail clerks in labor disputes explains, "Most of the grievances that come up remind me of my worst days in junior high school; life as a grocery store clerk seems to be defined by back-biting and gossip, cliques of the popular and the unpopular, rumors of illicit romance, favoritism, and the petty and vindictive authority of the—generally not terribly bright—store manager. All very petty and parochial and depressing."

A Wal-Mart worker in the Northeast, a woman who was tormented mercilessly by her coworkers about her weight and personal hygiene—almost as if they were still in junior high—characterized the same environment in a succinct phrase: "Management by gossip." Employment lawyers, social scientists, and many workers agree: discrimination flourishes in workplaces with murky performance criteria. Wherever personal feelings are allowed to prevail over job performance, women and minorities tend to suffer, along with any other workers who are marginal, whether because they are too outspoken, overweight, weird, or otherwise different or disliked. Few retail workplaces are entirely free of this problem.

Wal-Mart makes much of other companies' problems in its defense in *Betty Dukes et al. v. Wal-Mart Stores, Inc.,* pointing out often that all retailers have gender-based pay and promotion disparities in their workforces. During the class certification hearing, Wal-Mart's lead counsel, Nancy Abell, admitted that there are differences in pay between employees, mostly female, who sell clothing and those who sell hardware or sporting goods—mostly male. She pointed to disparities throughout the industry and argued that Wal-Mart has to pay "according to the market. . . . Our store managers must respond to the real world." In fact, as the industry leader, Wal-Mart has tremendous power to define the "market" and to reshape the "real world." Anwar Shaikh, an economist who teaches at the New School University, has argued that in most industries, one firm sets the terms by which all its competitors must operate. In the retail industry, that company is certainly Wal-Mart. In any event, the fact that other companies are also sexist is not a legally acceptable defense—but it does help to put the workers' experience in context and suggests that the *Dukes* lawsuit could have a dramatic impact if it encourages other workers to bring suits, and other companies to reform their practices.

It is clearly possible for a retailer to be far more woman-friendly than Wal-Mart and still be very successful. Minneapolis-based Target Stores is *Fortune* magazine's second most admired general merchandiser, after Wal-Mart. As with Wal-Mart, a large majority of its employees—67 percent—are women. But unlike Wal-Mart, nearly 50 percent of Target's salaried managers are women. At Target, which in addition to its Target stores also owns Marshall Field's and Mervyn's California, women hold half the senior executive posts. Women also hold high-profile positions as president (of Marshall Field's and Mervyn's, as well as Target Brands), VP of investor relations, and senior VP of finance. Three out of four regional vice presidents are women, as well as four of the company's fourteen directors.

Target shouldn't be idealized, however, because it isn't a great employer. The company is not unionized, though a handful of employees have been trying to organize. In many markets its wages are as low as Wal-Mart's. Just like Wal-Mart, Target forbade workers from discussing wages with one another, before the National Labor Relations Board declared the policy illegal. The Equal Employment Opportunity Commission has accused Target of race discrimination, and its former parent company, Dayton Hudson, was banned for 14 years from doing business with the city of Minneapolis for refusing to submit to affirmative action plans (as all companies in Minneapolis must do to be eligible for public subsidies).

Despite these failings, Target is widely recognized as a nonsexist employer for women. For three years in a row it has been named by *Latina Style* magazine as one of the 50 best companies for Latinas to work for. The magazine noted the benefits and special efforts to promote women, as well as the fact that women and Hispanics serve on the board of directors.[2] As of 2003, Target had made *Working Mother* magazine's list of 100 Best Companies for working mothers for nine years running, the only major retailer besides Sears to achieve that distinction. (Indeed, Sears became a much better employer for women after a major lawsuit in the seventies and eighties.) "If you're executive material, it's a good bet you'll be groomed to climb at this mega-retailer, where women are encouraged to make their way to the upper ranks," raved the magazine, noting that Erica Street, president of Target Brands, is a working mother. *Working Mother* also pointed out that hourly workers may choose their schedules, and that the company has flextime and a Reasonable Time Off program, which makes it easy for workers to change schedules for personal reasons. The company's female-friendliness has also been recognized by *Business Ethics* magazine, which has praised Target as one of its "100 Best Corporate Citizens," specifically citing women in prominent leadership positions, discounts at community child-care centers, and family flexibility, including 20 weeks of maternity leave. Target has also been praised for the quality of training offered to its employees, a huge benefit to women. Coleman Peterson, the head of Wal-Mart's People Division, admitted in a deposition that he had written a memo in which he cited Target's record to show his Wal-Mart colleagues that they could do better in promoting women.

In an industry characterized by sex discrimination, Target—headquartered in progressive Minneapolis—is clearly an exception. Target also spends time and money on its human resources department, and consciously promotes an antisexist environment. It boasts a cutting-edge image nurtured by playful, MTV-inspired television ads and clothing designs by Isaac Mizrahi, which no doubt attracts the sort of liberal-minded managers who are less likely to tolerate primitive gender attitudes. Differences between Wal-Mart and Target may also have something to do with their markets: Target pursues a young, hip, more urban consumer, who tends to have more liberal social attitudes than the older, more rural Wal-Mart customer. Unfortunately, Wal-Mart, which has more than five times as many workers as Target, affects many more women's lives, and because it is so hugely successful it has many more imitators in the industry.

Past class-actions against retailers have resulted in modest institutional changes. The charges in these suits were similar to those in *Dukes v. Wal–Mart*, but because of its scope and scale *Dukes* has far more potential to affect the industry, and greater political and social significance. It is worth looking at some of its predecessors, because they give us an idea of what can be accomplished.

The first major sex discrimination suit in the retail industry was *Equal Employment Opportunity Commission v. Sears, Roebuck*, filed in federal court in 1979. At Sears stores, men dominated the big-commission sales jobs, selling electronics or household appliances, while women barely eked out minimum wages as hourly sales clerks in lower-paying departments. Between 1973 and 1980, women made up 75 percent of Sears's noncommission sales force and only 27 percent of commission salespeople. Hourly earnings for commissioned workers in their first year were twice those of noncommission-sales workers. In the early 1970s, the Equal Employment Opportunity Commission (EEOC) made many attempts to get Sears—at that time, the nation's largest retailer—to voluntarily reform its practices but, in the government's view, the company made few meaningful changes. Finally, in 1979, the EEOC filed a lawsuit against Sears charging discrimination in hiring and promotions under Title VII of the Civil Rights Act of 1964. The retailer immediately doubled the number of commissioned saleswomen, but decided to fight the charges in court. Sears argued that women preferred the lower-paying jobs because they weren't interested in the dog-eat-dog competition salespeople endured in the commission jobs. Ultimately that argument prevailed, and the EEOC lost its case in 1988.

In a mistake that plaintiffs' lawyers would be unlikely to make today, the EEOC attorneys relied entirely on statistics, presenting no examples of actual women who had been harmed by Sears's practices. The court reprimanded the EEOC for presenting no plaintiffs or anecdotal evidence that might have brought "cold numbers convincingly to life."[3] Government lawyers insisted that given the scale and scope of the discrimination they were describing, anecdotes would be meaningless.[4] Within such a large organization, they reasoned, anyone might experience anything—and certainly there would be women who could credibly claim they had not suffered discrimination—so the salient story lay in the data. The same could be said of Wal-Mart, of course, but courts have generally insisted that numbers are inadequate, because it is not enough to prove discrimination: plaintiffs must show that the defendant's actions hurt real people. In the court's eyes, if a woman didn't notice she was being discriminated against, then it never happened. Since the government's disastrous defeat in *EEOC v. Sears,* plaintiffs' lawyers have heavily emphasized women's stories.

To many observers—especially those on the political right—the fact that the EEOC spent so many years on a losing case confirms its reputation as a wasteful, ineffective government bureaucracy. Ironically, the right-wing Supreme Court justice Clarence Thomas headed the agency for most of the duration of the Sears case. Indeed, the EEOC was famously inefficient during this period; most observers agree it has been slightly better in every subsequent administration, despite being seriously underfunded by both Republicans and Democrats. Critics now are far more likely to accuse the EEOC of political spinelessness—of not pursuing offending companies aggressively enough.[5] The agency has not been involved in the most high-profile discrimination cases, including *Dukes v. Wal-Mart.*

The "lack of interest" argument used by Sears—which Wal-Mart has flirted with by presenting data showing that women are selected for promotion more often than they apply—has been a powerful one in sex discrimination cases because, as the legal scholar Vicki Schultz has argued, courts and companies alike assume that women's work preferences are formed in childhood by the wider culture before they even get to the workplace, and plaintiffs' lawyers have usually failed to challenge that view. She writes: "The lack of interest argument attacks the meaningfulness even of statistical evidence showing egregious, long-standing patterns of segregation. For if these patterns are the expression of women or minorities' independent work preferences, then employers cannot be blamed."[6] Schultz argues that plaintiffs will be more successful in countering the "lack of interest" argument when they show that preferences are shaped on the job, and that the employer can play an active role in affecting women's aspirations. If *Dukes* goes to trial, it seems likely that the plaintiffs will make some version of Schultz's argument, since evidence of Wal-Mart's sexist culture has already been important in the case.

In recent years, some of the major successful sex discrimination suits against retail companies have been litigated by

Betty Dukes's lawyer, Brad Seligman. The biggest of these was *Stender v. Lucky Stores*, filed in 1988 on behalf of 14,000 women who had worked for a (now-defunct) West Coast grocery chain. Like the *Dukes* women, the *Stender* plaintiffs said they were steered into low-paying, hourly jobs, and rarely were promoted into management. U.S. District Judge Marilyn Patel ruled in favor of the plaintiffs in August 1992, finding that the company permitted highly subjective personnel practices, and made unsupported assumptions about women's ambitions (the time-honored "lack of interest" premise). The following month, Lucky Stores and the plaintiffs worked out a consent decree, subject to supervision by the court, in which the company agreed to make up for past discrimination by meeting certain quotas for the promotion of women.

The consent decree also set guidelines that Lucky Stores had to follow in making initial assignments, determining hours, moving employees from part-time to full-time positions, and deciding on promotions and training. Lucky Stores agreed to rigorously document its practices and to institute specific policies on the resolution of complaints, job posting, and management training and evaluation.

In 1993, Lucky agreed to pay nearly $75 million in damages: $1.2 million to the six named plaintiffs (the representatives of the class), $59.1 million to be distributed among the 14,000 class members, and $13.7 million for plaintiffs' legal fees. (This was one of the settlements that later helped Seligman to start the Impact Fund.) A class member's individual cut could range from $100 to $10,000, depending on her seniority and how much of her potential earnings she'd lost to Lucky's discrimination. On top of that, the company agreed to invest an additional $20 million in affirmative action programs for female employees, and to pay an additional $13 million if it failed to meet court-ordered targets for hiring and promotion. At that time, the combined total cost of the settlement to Lucky made it the second-largest sex discrimination settlement in history, second only to the $240 million State Farm had to pay in 1992 to settle *Krasewski v. State Farm* (an amount since surpassed by a $508 million settlement paid by Voice of America in 2000).

Seligman and four of the named plaintiffs were ebullient at a press conference announcing the *Stender v. Lucky Stores* settlement. "Lucky's main defense was that women are not as interested in promotions as men," Seligman said. "We always wondered how Lucky knew that."[7] One named plaintiff, Diane Skillsky, had worked for many years as a checker in Redwood City, and saw her son, who had begun as a checker, promoted into a management-training program years before she was allowed into management. Another plaintiff, Irma Hernandez, said of a former supervisor, "If you slept with him, you were promoted."[8]

The suit led to long-lasting change at Lucky Stores. A decade earlier, only 3 percent of Lucky's managers were women, although women made up 40 percent of its workforce. After the lawsuit and subsequent consent decree, 58 percent of management jobs went to women.

Soon after the Lucky settlement, Atlanta-based Home Depot, the nation's largest home-improvement chain, faced a similar lawsuit, *Butler v. Home Depot*. The company's western division was the target of a class-action suit filed in 1994 in the Ninth Circuit Court, which grew out of more than 60 individual claims. The class included 17,000 female employees in 150 stores, in 10 western states. The plaintiffs charged discrimination in pay training and promotions: women were routinely assigned to the cashier jobs that, unlike the sales positions, presented little opportunity for promotion. Seventy percent of Home Depot's sales jobs were held by men, and 70 percent of the cashiers were women. Ninety-four percent of the store managers were men.

The lead plaintiff was Vicki Butler who, before working at a Sacramento Home Depot, had been an Air Force mechanic, a greenhouse manager, and a general home repairwoman. Home Depot hired her as a cashier when she had the experience to work on the sales floor, and then promoted a younger, less experienced man over her.

Home Depot used the "lack of interest" defense, arguing that women apply for the cashier position and are not interested in sales. The company also asserted that it preferred its salespeople to have construction experience, which women did not tend to have. This position was undermined by one of the plaintiffs, Kathleen York, who had been assigned to the cash register even though her previous job had been in a lumberyard. "Girls do not work in lumber," she was told.[9]

Butler v. Home Depot was settled just three days before trial in 1998. Home Depot admitted no wrongdoing but, in a consent decree intended to be in force for five and a half years, agreed to pay $87.5 million to the plaintiffs and to reform assignment and promotion practices throughout the company's nationwide operations, not just in the division directly charged in the suit. As a direct result of this class action, Home Depot's promotion process became more formal. The company began posting its jobs nationwide, and introduced a new requirement that management must interview at least three people for a job—fairly easy and standard practices.

The company has been stingy with information about this settlement, so it has been difficult for anyone to report on it fully, but the lawsuit seems to have made the company a modestly better place for women to work. In the western division, the female sales force increased by 37.5 percent between 1996 and 2000, and a similar increase took place in Home Depot stores nationwide, reports Michael Selmi, a George Washington University law professor and a scholar of class actions who has studied the case.[10]

Yet the settlement agreement provided no specific goals for promoting the women who had experienced past discrimination, and the company made no effort to offer jobs to women who had been discriminated against and offered only monetary compensation. No diversity task force was created, though an African American female board member was given the responsibility of overseeing the settlement agreement.[11] Home Depot failed to meet many of its own goals for improvement and, in a move Selmi calls "extraordinary," the parties filed a joint motion to close out the consent decree 18 months early. Of this action, Selmi said in an e-mail exchange, "Any judge who was reviewing the matter with any care would not have signed it. . . . Home Depot provided the least amount of information on a class action suit that I have seen." But, he added, judges don't usually care much about this last stage of a lawsuit. "She likely had very little interest in the actual outcome. . . . [M]ost judges will be happy to sign off on whatever the parties bring once the case is settled."

In evaluating the failures of the Home Depot suit, Selmi surmises that the company felt little pressure partly because the suit attracted so little media attention. Unlike Wal-Mart, Home Depot isn't a much-discussed company and the allegations were routine sex discrimination charges, which trouble the public far less than, for example, lurid racial epithets such as those that came to light in the course of the lawsuit against Texaco (*Roberts v. Texaco*). The accomplishments of *Butler v. Home Depot* shouldn't be dismissed, but it's clear that the company could have been forced to do much more if the judge had been more involved and the plaintiffs' lawyers had been far more aggressive in enforcing the consent decree.

The disappointing outcome of the Home Depot case is not that unusual. Sadly, class actions often do little to alter the status quo. In his 2003 study of discrimination suits, "The Price of Discrimination: The Nature of Class Action Employment Discrimination Litigation and Its Effects," Selmi writes that settlements in class actions "frequently produce little to no substantive change within corporations."[12]

The settlements are peanuts for these large companies— even in a record-breaking race discrimination settlement, Coca-Cola had to pay only .15 percent of the value of the company's stocks and bonds—$193 million. But in addition, Selmi found in his study, most suits had no significant impact on companies' stock value. Selmi's findings suggest that class actions may not even do enough damage to a company to act as a deterrent. The institutional reforms mandated in settlements generally took a backseat to monetary damages, Selmi found, with the result that the company's discriminatory practices continued. He observed that preventing future discrimination was rarely a priority of the court: "For firms, discrimination claims are now like accidents—a cost of doing business, which necessarily implies that a certain level of discrimination will persist. . . . It appears that as a society we no longer desire to eradicate discrimination, but instead have placed a price on it."[13]

Part of the reason for this, writes Selmi, is that courts don't get involved enough in the oversight of reforms, as happened in the Home Depot case. Class actions are fairly unique in the legal system, in the level of court supervision required after litigation is over, and many judges don't step up to the plate. As a result, the lawsuits often don't force corporations to change their ways, and "whatever changes occur tend to be driven by a company's own interests or by public relations concerns rather than the requirements of a consent decree."[14]

Enforcement has become privatized, as Selmi observes; the government largely leaves follow-up to the plaintiffs' lawyers, or to "diversity consultants" hired by the company. When judges abdicate responsibility, the public interest in their outcome goes largely unrepresented, despite the fact that public money has been spent litigating these cases, which are heard in public courtrooms.

In the case of *Dukes v. Wal-Mart,* it's difficult to know what the prospects would be for effective monitoring and enforcement of any settlement. The case has already received considerably more media attention than *Butler v. Home Depot* did, and that could shame Wal-Mart into making major changes. It may help, too, that the suit is being litigated by a coalition that includes nonprofit public interest groups like the Impact Fund and Equal Rights Advocates at great cost to their organizations. The public-interest groups cannot profit from the case, and have taken it on solely because they want to change Wal-Mart. Most class actions are litigated by a single for-profit law firm; certain lawyers may individually have idealistic motives but, with so much money to be made by the law firm, attorneys and firms don't always put the public interest first. *Dukes v. Wal-Mart* also has the advantage of being a landmark case—no one has had to reform a company of this size, with such an entrenched problem, ever before—which should appeal to the egos of the plaintiffs' attorneys: they have an opportunity to truly make their mark on the retail industry.

Where Selmi worries that class-action suits don't bring about institutional change, others worry that they don't even help individual workers. Deborah Calloway, at professor at the University of Connecticut Law School and an expert on employment discrimination, says of the potential *Dukes* class action, "You have to understand, this is not necessarily beneficial for the plaintiffs." Damages in class actions are split among the class members, with the result that often, a plaintiff with an "awesome claim" receives far less money than if

she'd brought an individual suit. Class members in employment class-action settlements typically get about $10,000
each, whereas an individual bringing a suit could take home
several million. "It never works out quite right," Calloway
says. "The poor woman who is entitled to a lot is getting half
that, and someone else who wasn't entitled to a darn thing is
going to get something, and nobody gets quite the right
thing. . . . It is never quite fair for the individual [class] members. " Besides, she says of *Dukes*, "with a class this large, a lot
of [women] are never going to figure out that they're in it." If
the class ends up covering all women who worked at Wal-
Mart after December 26, 1998—1.6 million women—telling
workers, especially those no longer working for the company,
about it will pose a tremendous mass communication challenge. To Calloway, in large class-action suits, "the biggest
winners are the lawyers."

The workers are not in control of these lawsuits, for the
lawyers make most of the significant decisions. Class actions,
although they can win institutional reforms that improve
conditions for workers, do not substantially challenge power
relations between worker and boss. That's probably why,
in areas of the country where class actions are particularly
common, these suits do not give the poor any more social
power than they have anywhere else. Mississippi, known as
"Tortsissippi," is the bête noire of conservatives who regard
class-action suits as a serious threat to free-market capitalism.
Mississippi courts are among the most plaintiff-friendly
in the nation. Alan Huffman, a Mississippi writer, describes
one of its regions, Jefferson County, as a "victim-based econ-

omy" in which entire towns, lacking genuine industry, are kept afloat by individuals who have prevailed in large class-action settlements.[15] What is tragic about this situation is not the assault of Mississippi courts on the rights of business-men, but what the state's experience suggests about the powerlessness of the American poor. Mississippi is one of the nation's poorest states, and instead of political power, which could be achieved by collective action and organizing, all its citizens are getting is damage control. A class-action suit can compensate individuals and perhaps force some lawyer-mediated structural changes on the company. But it cannot, in the long run, give workers more power, which is of course why Wal-Mart accepts class actions as a routine cost of doing business, but fights unions tooth and nail.

In an alarming indicator of the power large companies have in the United States, class-action suits, despite their insignificant impact on corporate profits, are widely viewed by conservatives and many media elites as too costly to companies. Generally, civil-rights class-action suits of all kinds have been on a long decline since at least 1976 (the first year that complete data were available on civil rights and employment rights cases filed in the United States), when there were about 2,000 such suits, and reached a low of 158 in 1991.[16] Employment class actions alone totaled 1,174 in 1976, and 39 in 1991. They've rebounded only modestly: in 2001, 238 civil-rights class actions were filed, 73 on behalf of workers.

One of the reasons for this is that class actions have been a consistent bugbear of the political right, which has painted plaintiffs and plaintiffs' lawyers as greedy opportunists and ignoring any potential public benefit to curbing corporate abuses. An increasingly conservative judiciary has often accepted these arguments, and government agencies like the EEOC have been compromised in their ability to bring them by lack of funds and, because of conservative ideologies, have been disinclined to do so anyway. As limited as the effects of many class-action suits may be, as far as conservative business interests are concerned, they are far too effective. In recent years, many laws have been passed to make it more difficult for ordinary people to sue corporations and win; for example, federally funded legal service lawyers are no longer allowed to bring class actions.

Even as *Dukes v. Wal-Mart* moved through the discovery phase in early 2003, Congress debated the so-called Class Action Fairness Act, which joins the Clear Skies Initiative and the Help America Vote Act in the pantheon of legislation designed to accomplish precisely the opposite of what its appealing name suggests. The Class Action Fairness Act would severely limit civil-rights class-actions suits, first, by moving all class-action suits currently in state courts to federal courts, which would overload the system so severely that it would take years for most of them to be heard, let alone resolved. (It already takes a long time: *Dukes v. Wal-Mart* was filed in 2001, and did not pass the certification phase until June 2004.) Even worse, the proposed law prevents plaintiffs from collecting more damages in a suit than any other class member, a serious disincentive for bringing a class action, given that a plaintiff in a class-action suit already collects less than she would if she brought an individual suit. In arguing for the legislation, Republicans have claimed that class actions are driving up the cost of doing business, and that companies are victimized by reckless juries who hand out increasingly large awards. A 2003 study that was conducted by the New York University Center for Law and Business found that the amount of money awarded to plaintiffs in such cases, including lawyers' fees, has held steady throughout the decade, and is not on the rise.[17]

The Class Action Fairness Act, which at this writing has passed the House but just died in the Senate, stalled at least for this season, would have had no effect on *Dukes v. Wal-Mart* because the case is already in federal court, and the plaintiffs' lawyers were already planning to follow many of the Act's procedural mandates anyway, such as court oversight of how much lawyers are paid, and giving notice to the class on important developments in the case. Joe Sellers explains, "We have, out of an abundance of caution, been going through a number of procedural steps in this case that are more expensive, more elaborate than normal because it's so big. We are trying very hard to minimize the ways in which anybody can challenge what we're doing." Still, even though the legislation has failed for now and would not in any case have affected *Dukes* directly, it is likely to resurface. If the Class Action Fairness Act is revived and passes, it will intensify the pro-business climate that discourages such actions, and greatly lessen the deterrent effect of a *Dukes* plaintiffs' victory.

Increasing costs for plaintiffs are also a factor in the decline of the civil rights class-action suit. Companies are bigger and more profitable than in the past, and they are willing and able to spend far more on litigation. The recent history of class-action litigation provides a sobering window on the growing power of capital over the public sphere, and the increased fragmentation, and even privatization, of reform efforts.

Women's advocates such as Kim Gandy, the president of NOW, frequently assert that Wal-Mart ought to stop discriminating against women because doing so is "bad for business." Unfortunately, there's little evidence that this is the case. Despite rampant sex discrimination, Wal-Mart is the most profitable company in the world. No studies support the notion that the market punishes companies for such behavior, which is an article of faith among orthodox economists and liberals. Since most people agree that ending race and sex discrimination is a good thing, there have been several empirical attempts to show that diversity policies affect profit but, so far, researchers have had to conclude that they do not.[18]

Laura Liswood, a senior adviser to Goldman Sachs on diversity, was—however euphemistically—right on target recently when she told *Workforce* magazine, "Typical profit and loss systems don't capture the benefits that diversity creates."[19] In other words, racism and sexism probably do not reduce profits, though of course it's a good idea to fight them for other reasons.

Wal-Mart is brilliant at making money. If social justice generated profit, Wal-Mart would have figured this out, and would not need feminists and public interest lawyers to tell it to clean up its act. That is precisely the challenge of changing Wal-Mart. Joe Sellers explains,

> Wal-Mart is about as good as any company, probably better, in tracking the aggregate results of various performance— you know, how many shoes you sell, what the temperature is in your store—they're very good at that, because those have economic consequences. They have not developed nearly to the same extent, the means, the databases, and the protocols for monitoring the performance of their managers [on diversity]. . . . They focus, for the most part, on their bottom line.

Women at Wal-Mart are also in a terrible labor-market position: it is not profitable for the company to listen to their complaints, because very often these workers have no exit strategy. Because Wal-Mart has so often put the local competitors out of business, women working at Wal-Mart often have few other potential employers. "They have no choice, if they want to remain in retail, [than] to work at the Wal-Mart, even if the working conditions are pretty abysmal," says Sellers. If Wal-Mart faced a shortage of workers, because of a revived economy or the emergence of better options for working-class women, the company would have to respond to problems like sex discrimination but, so far, that hasn't happened. "Wal-Mart has not seen a real economic incentive to treat people better," Sellers says.

Still, since Wal-Mart is the most important retailer in the world, the *Dukes* lawsuit has the potential to put all other

major chains on notice and have a serious impact on the retail industry. Dee Gunter says she hopes *Dukes* will "send a
message to all those other retailers who want to keep women
barefoot and pregnant."

Deborah Calloway, despite her qualms about class-action
suits, acknowledges that they have a major benefit that individual suits lack: the potential for public education. "What
would make [Wal-Mart] change," says Calloway, "is not the
cost of this lawsuit. That's a cheap way to buy off a lot of
claims. What is more likely to make them change is bad
press." A class-action suit does present a tremendous opportunity to educate the public on the company's crimes,
and chapters 6 and 7 will explore the ways in which women's
groups and labor advocates have sought to do that. But
media coverage has an effect inside the company as well:
many Wal-Mart employees say they learned about *Dukes* not
from management or coworkers, but from watching TV.
Given the limitations of class-action suits, *Dukes v. Wal-
Mart's* historic significance could lie in its capacity to inspire
Wal-Mart's employees' to do something even more revolutionary: organize.

6

WWJD?
ORGANIZE WAL-MART!

CLASS-ACTION SUITS can bring about some institutional changes and force companies to pay damages, but there is no substitute for reforms that give more power to the workers themselves. Unions are still among the few institutions capable of doing that. Some *Dukes* witnesses, deeply politicized by their experiences of sex discrimination at the company, have become convinced that Wal-Mart workers need a union. At this writing, not a single Wal-Mart store in the United States is unionized. Joyce Moody is hoping to change that.

Moody, now 49, worked for Wal-Mart for 23 years, beginning in 1977 in Ripley, Mississippi, near Ashland, where she grew up. It wasn't what she'd hoped to do with her life.

When I got out of high school, I was seventeen years old. My mom and dad, mostly my mom, was very strict, and I wanted to go to college. I wanted to go to a business college

in Memphis, Tennessee. And my mother. . . most parents are
excited that their kids want to go to college. . . . My mother
was, like, "You are not leaving home! You are not staying in
the dorm and I am not paying for this."

Moody tried beauty school but hated it. She dropped out
and went to work first at a Wurlitzer piano factory and then
a telephone factory, where she worked the night shift assembly line, putting the ringers in the phones. She left that job
when she got pregnant and stayed home for a few years with
her son, who is disabled. Moody didn't love being at home
full-time—"I was going stir crazy"—but she didn't want to
go back to factory work. "Wal-Mart was just opening up in a
little town about twenty miles away," she says. "I had told my
husband I wanted to go back to work. So I did."

Wal-Mart hired Moody on her twenty-third birthday, to be
part of the team that opened the new Ripley Wal-Mart store.
At first she worked in pets, then in hardware—"wherever I
was needed"—but just before opening day, she was made
department manager of health and beauty aids. She then left
Wal-Mart briefly; her marriage was in trouble, and she tried
to salvage it by moving with her husband to Memphis, where
he wanted to live. They divorced within the year, and Joyce
Moody returned to Mississippi with her son. She returned,
too, to Wal-Mart, this time working in its Corinth store as a
full-time hourly employee.

When she was married, Moody didn't need to work full-
time because her husband had a decently paying job in a
tool-and-dye factory. "I was really wanting just part-time,

something to get out of the house for a while," she says, but because of her divorce, the Wal-Mart job "went into full-time real fast."

Compared to factory work, which she found limited and isolating, Moody enjoyed retail, and for years she was happy working at Wal-Mart: "You know, you met new people every day. We had a lot of fun on the job. It wasn't as restrictive as working at a factory where you couldn't leave your area. . . . It was just the perfect job for me. I just stuck with it."

Even back in these good days, however, women weren't treated fairly, says Moody. She constantly asked managers in Corinth for promotions, but they wouldn't let her advance beyond the department-manager level. One store manager, Roy Flake, explained his failure to promote her by telling her she should be home taking care of her disabled son, not working.

Eventually she persuaded Flake to promote her into an office-training-supervisor job (still hourly, but better paid and more responsible than department manager), and in 1984, she got another promotion, to store planner, which is a salaried position. Keeping her home in Walnut, Mississippi, Moody would travel by car to stores as far away as Laramie, Wyoming, preparing workers at dozens of new stores for "grand openings." She and the other women on the store-planning team used to grumble about being paid less than the men. Moody's title was "office supervisor," like all the other women's, whereas all the men had the title "setup supervisor." Years later, in a deposition for *Dukes v. Wal-Mart*, she stated: "They made more money than what we did, and they had less responsibility than what we did. . . . There were always comments, with the guys telling us that they were our boss. We had to do what they told us to do, because they made more money. That was pretty constant at the time, even though we were supposed to have been on the same level."

Still, she loved the fast pace and constant change of the store-planning job, and threw herself into it until 1990, when she tired of life on the road and of the long hours. Moody asked to return to Mississippi, and accepted an assistant-manager job back in the old familiar Corinth store. At first it felt like a delightful homecoming. But she found that things had changed.

The paternalistic sexism she'd dealt with in her early days in Corinth had been irritating, but at least people had been friendly. Now, a new district manager, Bill Wulfers, behaved as though he positively despised the women working under him. "It wasn't just me," she recalled later in a deposition. "He treated the other lady assistants in the district pretty much the same way." He either ignored them or was verbally abusive, though he was friendly with the male managers.

Wulfers made it clear he did not want any "lady assistant managers" in his district. He hassled Moody endlessly. "He even told me that I should transfer to a district four to five hundred miles north of where I was currently working if I wanted to remain an assistant manager," said Moody in her class-member statement. When she said she didn't want to move her family after being on the road for so long, Wulfers hung up on her.

One might hope that Wulfers's difficulty working with women would have hurt his career—but not at Wal-Mart. He rose through the ranks and in August 2001, after 14 years with the company, become senior vice president of the company's southeast division.

Moody resigned from her Corinth position just a month after she was hired. Four female coworkers, all of whom had been ill-treated by Wulfers, approached her, asking if she wanted to join them in filing a charge against Wal-Mart with the Equal Employment Opportunity Commission. Moody refused. She says now that she was concerned about the other women's futures: "I still thought they might have a career with the company and I did not want to jeopardize that for them," she says. "They depended on Wal-Mart for their livelihood."

She may have been looking out for her own career, too. Though Moody hoped not to return to Wal-Mart, she kept her options open in her resignation letter, writing, "If at any future date I could return, I would like reconsideration in taking me back." In fact, after looking for work for more than four months and finding nothing, she did go back to work at Wal-Mart, this time moving to the Bentonville headquarters to work as a merchandise coordinator in the home office—an hourly position. "I still believed in the company," she says. "I still wanted to be part of it."

Moody was promoted to a salaried merchandise-manager position in 1992, after less than two years at headquarters. The following year, she was told her position was being eliminated owing to a department "restructuring." Actually, the department was expanding, and her job wasn't eliminated, but instead was given to a male colleague, while Moody was demoted to an hourly job answering the employee hotline. She had just bought a house, expecting that she'd continue to earn a management salary.

During her time as an hourly worker in Bentonville, Moody experienced something many Wal-Mart workers complain about—she was asked to work "off the clock," that is, overtime that she was not paid for. Along with workers in more than 30 states, she has joined a class-action suit against Wal-Mart on that issue.

Moody worked her way back up, becoming a buyer's assistant, then a district manager for the Shoes and Jewelry Division. She noticed that most Shoes and Jewelry Division district managers were women, and that they made far less money than the other district managers.[1] Moody's observations are confirmed in the report submitted by the expert witness, Richard Drogin. Still, the position enabled her to return to her native Mississippi, to Walnut, her hometown, and she was happy about that. After she'd been there less than a year, Moody was ordered by the regional manager, Cindy Marsh, to move to the Mississippi Delta, which was the center of the district (comprising Mississippi and parts of Arkansas), if she wanted to keep her job. She had recently been car-jacked in the Delta area and she felt it was too dangerous. She didn't know of any male district managers who'd ever been required to make such a move. To avoid making the move, she gave up the district-manager position and began working as the manager of the Tire and Lube Express

(TLE) department of the Collierville, Tennessee, Wal-Mart, three hours from the Mississippi border. It was a mortifying step down: though she did not have to take a pay cut, the job carried significantly less responsibility and status. The man who took her district-manager job was not required to move to the Delta.

Her district manager in Collierville, Jeff Avant, would tell Moody—not the male employees—to clean the stockroom or the pit. "I would be told, 'The pit needs a woman's touch,'" Moody recalls. The "pit" is "where they change oil. . . where they drain the oil pan. And it's messy down there. You're talking about oil and filters. . . and stuff like that. And he tells me it needs a 'woman's touch.' I guess he wanted me to get the mop and the Clorox and scrub it, I don't know, put curtains on the wall or something," jokes Moody, still amazed at this incident. "If he could've seen my house he wouldn't have said that!"

Moody got fed up with such comments, and with being singled out for unpleasant tasks that men weren't asked to do. She asked to be transferred to New Albany, Mississippi, where she again ran the TLE department. But the environment there was even worse. In New Albany, she worked under District Manager James Harston. One day Harston came into the store, and Moody told him she wanted to speak with him—she had heard he was planning to lay off some workers in her department and she hoped, if at all possible, to protect their jobs. He asked her to take a ride in his car and she agreed. As they were driving, Harston, rather than discussing the layoffs, asked if she'd ever want to be a district manager again. Somewhat cautiously, not sure why he was asking, Moody said she would, but that she knew her department needed to reach certain sales numbers if she were ever to be promoted again.

"I'll help you if you'll help me," said Harston. She wasn't sure exactly what he meant, but his tone made her uncomfortable. Moody responded in her best brisk, business-like manner that all she needed was support in the business and she would be fine. Harston immediately took offense, and angrily turned the car around. The two drove back to the store in complete silence.

Harston's hostile reaction immediately confirmed what Moody had feared—the district manager had been coming on to her, and wouldn't accept rejection easily. Back in the store, Harston continued to take revenge on Moody, "singling me out for abusive tirades," she later testified. When she requested days off he denied them without giving any reason. Moody suffers from rheumatoid arthritis and wears a hand brace, which Harston told her "didn't look good"— he wanted to move her to a position where the public couldn't see her.

Moody's then fiancé (now her husband), David Moody, is a former Wal-Mart manager as well (he was fired from the company, he says, wrongfully). Before coming to Wal-Mart he had worked in a steel plant, where he helped to organize a union. Seeing the troubles Joyce was having at Wal-Mart, he wondered what union could give her advice about her rights. He went on the Internet and did some research, and learned that the United Food and Commercial Workers

Union (UFCW) had started a campaign to organize Wal-Mart workers nationwide, a campaign that Wal-Mart has virulently resisted.

The UFCW, the largest private-sector union in the United States (it represents one in nine U.S. union members), resulted from the 1979 merger of the Retail Clerks International and the Meat Cutters unions. Since the merger, it has helped its members, especially workers in grocery stores, win and keep excellent wages and benefits, but it has had tremendous difficulty adapting to a changing industry, and to the harsher market conditions imposed by large retailers, especially Wal-Mart. In a time when private-sector unions are shrinking dramatically—they now represent only 8 percent of private-sector workers—the UFCW's difficulties in organizing Wal-Mart have been of great concern to the labor movement.

At David's urging, Joyce called the union's headquarters in Washington, D.C., and spoke briefly to Vice President Al Zack, just to get some advice about the harassment from Harston. She wouldn't leave her name: she was terrified that Wal-Mart might find out she had called, and she wasn't sure, in any case, that she wanted anything further to do with the union. Like any Wal-Mart manager, Moody had attended numerous meetings in which her superiors denounced unions. "I never thought twice about a union. 'You don't need anybody to speak for you,'" managers would say in the meetings.

When Moody complained about the harassment to Scott McCarter, the regional personnel manager, he told her to "be the bigger person in the situation," and to try to "communicate better" with Harston.

Livid at this pathetic response, Moody resigned on the spot. Later, she changed her mind, because she still needed the job. "You say things in the heat of the moment that you really don't mean," Moody explains. Despite Moody's 23 years of service and her efforts to reconcile with the company, Wal-Mart fired her in January 2001. She says a man "probably fifteen to twenty years younger" than her took her job. "Twenty-three years, I mean, I grew up in Wal-Mart. I was devastated," she says now. "I was traumatized. . . . I just couldn't believe the company would do that to a longtime associate."

Like so many other women, Moody hopes to change Wal-Mart, and that is why she decided to become a witness in *Dukes et al. v. Wal-Mart Stores, Inc.* "The main thing that I hope is accomplished by this class-action suit is I hope more women are promoted based on their abilities," she says. "I hope that once they are promoted that they are paid the same as the men that are in the same position doing the same job."

Yet class-action suits alone do not give women, or any other workers, a voice on the job. Joyce Moody knows this, and is determined not only to sue Wal-Mart but to organize its workers. She had always believed what she was told by Wal-Mart: that Wal-Mart workers don't need unions because of the company's "Open Door" policy, whereby employees supposedly are encouraged to bring complaints to any superior at the company, at any level. But when she used the "Open Door" policy, she was first insulted, and then fired.

A month after Moody was fired by Wal-Mart, she and her husband began working as full-time organizers for its worst enemy—the UFCW. Joyce Moody realized she was furious not only about her own treatment but also about the company's harsh and inflexible treatment of the hourly workers. She realized that for years, as a manager, she'd had to make terrible, painful decisions. In mid-1990s, the company got much stricter about scheduling, "telling us, 'If they can't work when we need 'em, then we don't need 'em. You put out the schedule. If they can't work it then we'll find somebody else who can.' And I didn't like that."

Moody had also been in trouble over payroll, resisting Wal-Mart's practice of boosting a store's profits by cutting workers' hours:

> They would tell me, "You've got to cut so many hours this week," and, "You've got to come in under this percent or we're going to write you up." And I would call my people together, and I would say, . . . "I have to cut these hours. Do I have any volunteers?" I can honestly say I don't think I ever cut as many hours as they wanted me to. Because I knew those people were like me. They had bills, they had electricity, food, and I had been in their shoes before. So I wasn't going to take it away from them. Not with the company making billions of dollars a year. . . . I know that Wal-Mart has to keep their expenses down to make a profit, but it always falls on the associates, the hourly folks. Doesn't affect the managers' bonuses. They don't say, 'Well, we're gonna cut your bonus ten thousand dollars this year.'
>
> That's where the associates were getting so upset about their hours being cut. I mean, eight hours to them is a lot.

And the managers going around, "Well, I got a hundred-thousand-dollar bonus this year."

Moody was also furious about how little the hourly workers are paid—especially the women—many of whom had to receive public assistance, though they were working full-time. She says now,

> That's sad, the government had to pick up Wal-Mart's expenses. . . . Let [the company CEOs] stand in the Food Stamp line and see how it feels. I know, I've been there. When I started working with the company I was only making, I think, $2.79 an hour. That was back in '77. I had a son who was three years old. And his dad and myself had just divorced. And I was living in the projects. After all these years, I would like to see [Wal-Mart CEOs] David Glass or Lee Scott live on seven or eight dollars an hour.

The Moodys became a husband-and-wife organizing duo, spending most of their days driving from one small town to another, talking to Wal-Mart workers and trying to convince them to join the union. "Most of the time we're together twenty-four/seven," Joyce says. "We're a team in all aspects." Joyce feels that she and David have a cultural affinity with the workers that helps their organizing. "Most of the towns that we go into are rural America," she says. "And my husband and I both are from rural America. We talk to them one on one, and get them to feel comfortable with us."

When Joyce Moody talks with Wal-Mart workers, the topic of sex discrimination comes up frequently. She has given many women the 800 number of the *Dukes* plaintiffs' attorneys, and many of them have called. She has been organizing in Florida, Georgia, Alabama, North Carolina, South Carolina, Mississippi, and Tennessee. "I felt like the union would be able to help simply because the women would have a voice on the job," she says.

Gretchen Adams, the comanager who opened 27 Supercenters, working with men with little experience whose salaries far exceeded hers, says that in the beginning of her Wal-Mart career, she was completely "gung ho" about the company, more than willing to put in the 70-plus-hour workweek her job required. "I spent my life at Wal-Mart," she says. Adams used to lead anti-union meetings. They could always use the "Open Door" policy if they had complaints, she'd tell workers. "As a manager you have to believe that," she explains, "because you've got to convince others."

The sexism she encountered shook her faith in Wal-Mart, and opened her eyes to other problems with the company, especially the wages of the hourly workers. "They were not paid enough to live on. There were a whole lot of single mothers," she says. "They would come into my office crying their eyes out because they had hard decisions: whether to take their child to the doctor or pay their rent." She recalls "many, many times" having to sign paperwork so these women could collect Food Stamps. Adams sighs, thinking about how the company treated these workers—and her.

"So many inequities." Adams says she kept thinking she could make Wal-Mart a better company by working from the inside. "I kept asking myself, 'How can I change this?' But there wasn't any way I could personally change it." Once, Wal-Mart wanted her to fire 10 people in one week to boost the store's bottom line. "We didn't have to do that," she says now. "Where do you cut costs first? People. I thought, 'Isn't it wonderful what a 'family-oriented' company we are?'"

Adams's husband, watching her ordeal with the company, began telling her, "Wal-Mart needs a union."

"I'd say, 'Wash your mouth out with soap,'" she says, smiling wryly. But she came to think maybe he was right, and that even though what she wanted desperately was to be a Wal-Mart manager and treat workers well, perhaps she could do more good by joining the other side. A few months before she left Wal-Mart, she began talking to UFCW officials. "I realized, we had the same values," she says. "We could have a partnership." Her language strikingly evokes the idealism of many workers when they first come to work at Wal-Mart.

Adams quit Wal-Mart in December 2001. Like Joyce Moody, Adams is a *Dukes* witness who now works as an organizer with the UFCW. She still seems to sincerely regret the necessity of bringing the union into it. "It would be so much easier if Wal-Mart would step up to the plate" and treat people fairly, she says. Wal-Mart employees often tell her they don't need a union and can speak for themselves, reciting standard lines they've been fed from company propaganda sessions. During union drives, anti-union employees are given buttons that read, "I can speak for myself." Adams tells such Wal-Mart loyalists, "I've heard all that before. In fact, I know it better than you do—I used to teach people to say it." Such insider knowledge helps Moody and Adams anticipate Wal-Mart's strategies; they also relate to the employees better than a company outsider ever could.

Still, organizing Wal-Mart workers is hard, Moody says, because the company knows that workers live paycheck to paycheck and desperately need their jobs. "I just get really discouraged sometimes that people are so afraid to stand up to management. And I can understand. I've been on that side of the fence, where, you know, your livelihood pretty much depends on that job."

Still, Moody says, "I think eventually that there will be Wal-Mart stores that are unionized. I really do." She continues, "The associate at this point. . . doesn't trust Wal-Mart. . . . I'm not saying they trust me or the union one hundred percent, but they know it's got to be a change somewhere along the road, and they're willing to take that chance."

Moody knows she will never work at Wal-Mart again, joking, "If Wal-Mart becomes the only employer in the United States, I would be out of a job." Still, she is trying to unionize Wal-Mart for the same reason that she's suing the company for sex discrimination: to make it a better place to work—especially for women. "I don't hate Wal-Mart even today. I still think the company's good as a whole. But there's a lot of things that need to be fixed."

"I could've went in as one of these psychos," Moody says with a grim laugh, echoing many other Wal-Mart women who joked about identifying with ex-employees of the Post

Office and elsewhere who've gone on rampages in their former workplaces. "But I thought, no, what goes around comes around," she says. . . . I just feel for the people that are still there that are still being treated the way I was. Hopefully it'll change."

When it comes to sex discrimination, unions have not always been on the side of progress. Equal Rights Advocates (ERA), one of the organizations litigating *Dukes v. Wal-Mart*, frequently sues trade unions for excluding women. Such exclusion is one of the many reasons working-class women have such poor employment options in the first place and end up working at Wal-Mart. Even in the twenty-first century, many women are shut out of union-run apprentice programs and so they have trouble getting into skilled trades or carpentry, where the pay and benefits are far better than in retail.

Despite the discriminatory records of many unions, there is substantial evidence that a union could improve the lives of Wal-Mart's female employees. A study on women in the retail food industry, published in February 2002 by the Institute for Women's Policy Research (IWPR), a nonprofit public policy research organization, found that women retail workers gained significantly from union membership.[2] The study found that unionized women working full-time earned 31 percent higher wages than their counterparts who did not belong to unions, averaging $9.68 per hour to nonunion members' $7.39. If a woman works as a cashier—as more than half the women in the retail food industry do—she benefits especially from joining a union: unionized cashiers make $10.20 an hour, while nonunionized cashiers barely eke out a living at $6.72.

In addition, the study showed that two thirds of women in unionized retail jobs had health insurance, whereas only one third of nonunion women did. The unionized employers made higher contributions to women's pension and health plans. Single mothers benefitted more from union membership than other workers, and women working part-time gained more than full-time workers.

Especially significant was the finding—confirming the instincts of women like Joyce Moody—that among the unionized retail workers, the wage gap between men and women is smaller. Other studies have confirmed that women in unions face smaller gender wage gaps, and smaller race gaps between women of color and nonminority women.

Statistics collected by the U.S. Department of Labor on the workforce as a whole support these findings. Women represented by unions earn over 17 percent more than nonunion women. Furthermore, union women are closer to achieving parity with union men than nonunion women with nonunion men: unionized men earn about 23 percent more than unionized women, but nonunion men earn 28 percent more than nonunion women.

The *Dukes* plaintiffs' lead counsel, Brad Seligman, who has litigated sex discrimination suits against unionized supermarkets as well as nonunion retailers like Wal-Mart, agrees that a union can help prevent discrimination. Where there is a union, the hourly workers "are not completely helpless. Even if it's a weak union, at least there's somebody there who can file a grievance, who can do something." At nonunionized stores like Wal-Mart, the discrimination is worse and women are far less likely to be promoted. Although unionized and nonunionized supermarkets have about the same total numbers of male and female employees, 40 to 50 percent of managers at unionized grocery stores are female, in contrast to just 33 percent at Wal-Mart.

The story of unions' struggle to organize Wal-Mart is one of periodic momentum and enthusiasm. It takes place in a context of organized labor's declining numbers and diminishing political power, especially in the private sector. Unions view organizing Wal-Mart as a struggle for their survival: the success of such a deeply anti-labor company is a powerful symbol of their own relative powerlessness. To unionize it would completely transform organized labor's currently dismal position in this country. "Wal-Mart is the juggernaut," says one organizer. So far, however, the attempt to organize Wal-Mart has, in the United States, been a total failure.

Wal-Mart has been famously anti-union since Sam Walton's day. Beginning in the late 1980s, the UFCW began to realize that Wal-Mart's rapid growth and competitiveness posed an urgent threat to their members' jobs in other retail businesses. The first 24-hour Supercenter that sold groceries in addition to the company's traditional range of goods opened in 1988, in Washington, Missouri. By the end of 2003, Wal-Mart had opened 1,430 Supercenters. Historically Wal-Mart's presence had been greatest in states in the South that had passed laws giving employees the "right to work" without joining a union. In those states, the union shop is replaced by the open shop, where union membership is completely voluntary. In "right-to-work" states, it is very hard to organize or to bargain. But as Wal-Mart grew, it encroached upon more traditionally unionized western and Northeastern regions. Soon, unionized supermarkets were losing market share to nonunionized Wal-Mart stores. Despite the obvious threat to unionized stores, the effort to unionize Wal-Mart was halfhearted until the late 1990s, when it became painfully obvious that Wal-Mart threatened the UFCW's very survival—and its members' hard-won middle-class lives.

In early 2004, grocery-store workers in California, who had been on strike for months over management's plans to cut health benefits, were forced to accept a vastly reduced health plan as supermarkets, anticipating competition from new Wal-Mart Supercenters throughout the state, refused to compromise with the union. Supermarkets all over the country have been lowering wages and decimating workers' health plans and, according to Russ Davis of Massachusetts Jobs With Justice, who has worked closely with grocery workers struggling to maintain their standard of living, "It's all about Wal-Mart."

The urgency of organizing Wal-Mart is also underscored by the fact that the company is driving down wages and benefits not only in the retail and grocery industries, but everywhere: suppliers and building contractors must lower their labor costs to do business with Wal-Mart, and perhaps worse, the company is providing a business model widely imitated by other corporations. Susan Phillips, UFCW International vice president and director of its Working Women's

Department, says that anytime any private-sector union in the United States today goes into negotiations, "It's like there's this invisible eight-hundred-pound gorilla sitting in the room at the bargaining table."

Gretchen Adams says this is one of the reasons she is so motivated to organize her former employer's workers: in addition to her own searing experiences, she's deeply troubled by Wal-Mart's effect on the economy as a whole. "What about our working-class people?" she asks. "I don't want to live in a Third World country." Working people should be able to afford "a new car, a house. You shouldn't have to leave the car on the lawn because you can't afford that forty-five-dollar part."

Wal-Mart has been far more intense, creative, and consistent in its efforts to remain anti-union than any union has been in its efforts to organize the company. A 1991 handbook given to managers in the company's distribution center in Greencastle, Indiana, adapted from literature produced by Bentonville headquarters, urged daily vigilance, exhorting, "Staying union free is a full time commitment. Unless union prevention is a goal equal to other objectives in the organization, the goal will not usually be attained." The handbook advised managers to talk to workers about unions' historic connections to the mob "underworld" and "infringement on individual job freedom," as well as the dangers of losing jobs during strikes.

Managers are expected to monitor workers' conversations constantly and former managers have reported being encouraged to spy on employees. Though there are legal limits to employer spying, it is quite possible to use surveillance to create an uneasy, intimidating atmosphere without actually breaking laws.

According to Kathleen MacDonald, who has tried to organize her co-workers, this is what happened in her Aiken, South Carolina, store. Throughout the union drive, the pro-union workers "were under surveillance, we were being spied on. My department manager was on me like fleas on a cat." He asked her what she thought about a union at Wal-Mart and she answered, "If you asked me six years ago if we needed one, I would have said no. But now I think we do." The department manager reported that conversation to the store manager. He watched her constantly, took note of who she spoke with and reported that as well to the store manager. MacDonald says that one of her coworkers attended the union meetings as a spy, and told management who was there and what was said. She learned the extent of management's spying when she took the company to the National Labor Relations Board, the federal agency in charge of enforcing labor laws. The NLRB did not find management at the Aiken Wal-Mart guilty of illegal surveillance of workers.

Managers are also expected to report any union activity to headquarters—even any conversation the slightest bit sympathetic to unions. At the first sign of danger from union activity in a store, Bentonville dispatches the company's "labor relations" team to the store in a company plane ("Air Walton"), often the very day the call comes in. Once there, the professional union busters hold mandatory meetings with the workers.

Managers often tell them that if they vote for the union, the store will close. That tactic is illegal, but it is not the only one of Wal-Mart's union-busting strategies that skirt the line of illegality, and even cross it. As the Greencastle, Indiana, distribution center's handbook to managers noted frankly, during a union drive, "You. . . are expected to support the company's position and you may be asked to be a campaigner for the company. This may mean walking a tightrope between legitimate campaigning and improper conduct." Wal-Mart literature warns managers against threatening workers with job loss or shutdown, or firing them for union organizing—both of which are illegal. Yet the company has been fined by the NLRB for firing union sympathizers and for numerous other violations of freedom of association. For Wal-Mart, such fines are simply part of the cost of doing business, not a deterrent. Joyce Moody says she and David are honest with workers about the risks of organizing at Wal-Mart. "We don't guarantee them anything," she says. "And we certainly don't guarantee their jobs. Because my husband and I know very well that you can be terminated over anything."

Wal-Mart also keeps stores union-free by screening out union sympathizers in the application process. When Gretchen Adams was opening a new Supercenter in Las Vegas, the most unionized city in the United States, she "was not allowed to hire any experienced help, because they might be union." (She found this drastically affected the quality of applicants she could consider: "I end up teaching someone how to run a deli who didn't know how to read and write.") The company also administers personality tests to screen out those likely to be sympathetic to unions, and offers managers tips on how to spot such people. The Greencastle distribution center handbook urged managers to be wary of certain union-friendly types, including "the Cause-oriented Associate," who in high school "led demonstrations against everything from 'red dye' to 'ban the bomb.' He once took a trip to India to visit his personal 'guru.'" Another type to be wary of is the "Overly-qualified Associate. . . . a Ph.D. operating a grinding machine or a former accountant sweeping the floor. . . . This type of associate includes the associate who has formerly made substantially more money with other employers."

During the hiring process, many workers say, they have had to sign forms agreeing that they would not support any effort to unionize the store. Lorraine Hill, who worked in Wal-Mart stores in Rock Springs, Wyoming, and Oxford, Maine, had to do this in both stores. She says everyone did. "If you don't sign that paper you are not employed," she says. "It's not ethical. It's not legal. But if you are low income and you need the job, you abide by the rules."

In Germany and a few other countries, all retail workers are represented by a union, even Wal-Mart workers, but in the United States, only one group of Wal-Mart employees has successfully organized. In February 2000, ten meatcutters in a Jacksonville, Texas, Wal-Mart voted 7 to 3 to unionize their tiny bargaining unit. Two weeks later, Wal-Mart abruptly eliminated the meatcutters' jobs by switching to prepackaged meat and assigning the meatcutters to other departments, effectively abolishing the only union shop on its premises. The meatcutters filed a complaint against Wal-Mart with the National Labor Relations Board (NLRB). After more than three years, in June 2003—federal labor courts move slowly—an NLRB judge ruled Wal-Mart's move illegal and ordered the company to restore the department and recognize the meatcutters' bargaining unit. Wal-Mart has appealed that decision.

The UFCW's organizing effort goes beyond the workers themselves, to encompass the surrounding community. In Las Vegas, Linda Gruen, who worked at Sam's Club, was one of several workers cohosting a radio show devoted entirely to Wal-Mart's labor problems. Organizers have engaged not only other unions but also church groups in protests in Wal-Mart parking lots against sex discrimination, low wages, and heavy-handed union busting. A UFCW-organized Day of Action against the company in November 2002, inspired protests in more than 100 cities from Scarborough, Maine, to Waipahu, Hawaii. At a pre-protest pep rally in Grace Cathedral, a small Evangelical church at 886 Jerusalem Avenue in Uniondale, Long Island (an aptly named working-class and strongly union town), speaker after speaker told the crowd of mostly African American unionists, "Wal-Mart is going to take your job." As speakers enumerated the company's violations of labor rights in China and in the United States alike, loud murmurs of agreement swept through the church, giving it the feel of a revival meeting. Grace Cathedral's minister, R. W. Harris, whose congregation includes many Wal-Mart workers, told the crowd, "If Jesus were here today, he'd be at 886 Jerusalem Avenue with you."

The union has also focused on suing Wal-Mart for failing to pay workers overtime and violating workers' freedom of association. These suits heap bad press upon the company, and inspire some workers to stand up for their rights. Similarly, in many towns unions have joined forces with environmental activists and others to keep Wal-Mart from opening new stores; in California, significantly, the battle has centered on keeping the company from opening Supercenters, which are expected to destroy thousands of decent-paying grocery-store jobs. These efforts have been sporadically effective; a few Wal-Mart store openings have been averted, but many more communities can't resist the "low, low prices." One problem with union efforts to prevent store openings is that if a store does open anyway, Wal-Mart can then play on workers' fears, reminding them that if the union had its way, they wouldn't have these jobs. This can make organizing these workers almost impossible.[3]

Union organizers had long been aware that Wal-Mart was a women's issue, even before *Dukes v. Wal-Mart* was filed. In 1999 the UFCW's Working Women's Department organized nationwide Mother's Day protests in front of Wal-Mart stores in response to a study showing that, although two thirds of Wal-Mart's workforce were women, the company ranked last among retailers in equity and fairness. The protesters also noted a mounting series of individual sexual harassment and discrimination cases against Wal-Mart, and decried the company's threat to many women's better-paying jobs in other supermarkets. Under the slogan "Give Work-ing Moms a Real Gift: Don't Shop at Wal-Mart," union women picketed Wal-Mart stores, from City of Industry, California, to Peoria, Illinois to Utica, New York.

The UFCW doesn't do Mother's Day actions anymore be-cause Wal-Mart began to expect them, and to be prepared with rebuttals. But *Dukes v. Wal-Mart* has further encouraged the UFCW to focus on Wal-Mart's sex discrimination, which resonates with many women workers' personal experience. Not only have women like Gretchen Adams and Joyce Moody become union organizers because of sex discrimina-tion, but also the union drive has attracted the support of the National Organization for Women (NOW). UFCW and NOW members have passed out flyers in front of the stores to women workers, calling attention to pay and promotion disparities at Wal-Mart, and pointing out the role a union could play in bringing fairness to the company's women.

There is plenty of evidence that the company's sex dis-crimination prompts many women workers to look favor-ably upon the union. Only a few Wal-Mart workers have actually gone on the UFCW payroll as organizers, like Adams and Moody, but many more have tried to foster in-terest among their coworkers in their stores. MacDonald, who works in the Aiken, South Carolina, store, says that a few years ago, women at her store got fed up with the dis-crimination and thought seriously about a union. "We had tried the 'Open Door,'" and they had even complained to of-ficials from the Bentonville headquarters. "They wouldn't listen. They just ignored it. They shoved it under the rug." Women workers, many of them single mothers, were paid less than men for the same jobs, and were repeatedly passed over for promotions. Some employees had suggested, why not build a child-care center when Wal-Mart turned the store into a Supercenter? The company claimed it posed too many "insurance" problems.

Well and truly frustrated, MacDonald and her coworkers began holding meetings to plan a unionizing campaign. She had about 15 supporters, people who "said they wanted it and would stand beside me." But after her department manager ratted them out to management, "all hell broke loose." People came from the Home Office to show them anti-union movies. MacDonald faced retaliation: she and another pro-union worker were forbidden to speak to any other workers—on any subject—when they were on the floor, which is not legal, and made it difficult for them to do their jobs. She filed a charge with the NLRB against the company for violating her organizing rights. The NLRB ruled in September 2003, that Wal-Mart had indeed broken the law by giving MacDonald and her coworker a "no talking order." Wal-Mart's punishment was laughably slight: the company was ordered to obey the law in the future and to post a notice in the store letting employees know their organizing rights, and that store management had been found guilty of illegal union-busting tactics. The union attempt in the Aiken store had fizzled, but it did bring the workers a little closer to pay equality: "I did get a raise and other women got more money," MacDonald says, "so it wasn't a total loss."

The UFCW is attempting to organize Wal-Mart workers all over the country, and sometimes, as with the Texas meat-cutters, it comes close to victory. But mostly, when workers at Wal-Mart try to organize, the company intimidates them and they back down. "There's a lot of fear," says Linda Gruen, who tried for several years to organize her fellow Wal-Mart and Sam's Club coworkers in Las Vegas.

For the workers who do risk everything to organize, their coworkers' timidity can become frustrating. April Hotchkiss, the 22-year-old sales clerk in Pueblo, Colorado, is bursting with energy, anger, and determination to organize her coworkers, and is even publishing a newsletter to inform them about the benefits of unionization. She says many people support the union, but are afraid to play an active, outspoken role. MacDonald had similar experiences: people stood behind the union effort at first, but backed off when they saw how she was treated. "Now I know how Jesus felt," she jokes, but her sense of betrayal is real. For now, she has given up: "I think a lot of these people would sign a union card but they are afraid of losing their jobs and like I said these people are not used to sticking up for themselves. They resist change and are very naïve. . . . I am not going to stick my neck out for these people anymore."

Many women at Wal-Mart are afraid they will lose their jobs if they help organize a union, but would support it if their store had an election. One of those women is Betty

Dukes herself. "Would I vote for a union at Wal-Mart? Yes. Do I want to get fired over the issue? No." She laughs, adding, "Not yet." She is certain that if Wal-Mart had a union "there would be practically no discrimination," because a union would protect a complaining worker from retaliation, and force the company to address the issue.

Organizers must also confront the problem of low expectations. Because of their poverty and their profound identification with the company, "Many Wal-Mart workers think they have a pretty good deal," says Adams, incredulously. "But even some of the slaves thought they had it good."

Not all women who have suffered sex discrimination at Wal-Mart support the union. Many workers' perceptions of unions are dark to begin with, and Wal-Mart's propaganda campaigns are effective. Some current and former female managers feel—logically—that a union might not help their situation, as only nonmanagement workers can unionize.

One assistant manager in an Iowa store, who asked me not to use her name or city, says, "Wal-Mart is a sexist place." She worked for years in the railroad industry, which is quite male-dominated, and never encountered the kind of sex discrimination she's seen at Wal-Mart, where the salary of one male assistant manager who has been with the company for about the same amount of time is $10,000 more than hers. "I love him to death," she says, "but I have had to teach him almost everything." She feels men are favored extensively in her store, and says several female assistant managers have left for that reason. "To all of us women managers there seems to be a deliberate attempt to keep us second class," she says. She'd like to leave, but jobs in her region are scarce. Asked about unions, she jokingly recites the Wal-Mart line: "We are not anti-union, we are pro-associate," then explains her own opinion. "My personal view is that unions have very little place in a growth-oriented society. So, am I a good little Wal-Mart soldier? Sort of."

Of course, it would be unrealistic to expect all management women to adopt a pro-union position. Managers are trained to see unions as anathema to their own material interests.

But ambivalence and skepticism about unions at Wal-Mart persists even among hourly workers, and even among those hourly workers who have experienced sex and race discrimination. A jewelry department manager in Ohio, who believes she has experienced race and sex discrimination, says there was a lot of union activity at one Wal-Mart she worked in, before she got there. Despite her experiences, and her anger at the company, her feelings about unions are conflicted. Normally assertive and definitive, she frequently leaves sentences unfinished when discussing this subject. "I'm glad I wasn't there during the union drive," she says. "Too confusing. My husband is a union rep. He is always teasing me, 'Why don't you sign a card.' We don't talk about stuff like that. Well we do, but..."

She thinks for a moment, and clarifies her meaning. In addition to her husband's well-compensated union job, with ample benefits that she enjoys, the department manager looks favorably on her own union experience. "It was good when I worked in the post office," she observes. "For some companies, okay, but I know the stand Wal-Mart takes, and as long as I'm working for them. . . ." Micki Earwood, who worked briefly for the UFCW after being fired from Wal-Mart, knows what she means. Even though her father had been a union activist, Earwood says, in her early days at Wal-Mart, "My opinion was whatever they told me it was."

Chris Kwapnoski suffered 17 years of discrimination, 15 of them as an hourly worker; she could have used an advocate, and would have been eligible to join a union. Yet she feels strongly that a union is not needed at Wal-Mart. She says workers should be able to talk to managers when they have problems. "I have a big enough mouth," she says proudly, "I don't need anybody to speak for me," echoing the Wal-Mart propaganda that workers can "speak for themselves."

Kwapnoski's reaction to unions illustrates perfectly the way in which the ideology of individual rights can encourage women to take a stand against discrimination, but can also be deftly deployed by Wal-Mart to discourage unions and other forms of collective action. Many Wal-Mart workers are conservative, rural, and fundamentalist Christian, and are deeply attached to the ideal of American self-reliance.

Thus, these pervasive ideologies are a significant obstacle to organizing Wal-Mart, in addition to the sheer difficulty of fighting a company with so much money, anti-union zeal, successful propaganda, and a willingness to break the law.

New strategies may be needed to outmaneuver this company. Yet many labor organizers call the UFCW ineffectual, and they blame the union for its failure to organize Wal-Mart. To them, the UFCW simply does not have the creativity nor the determination necessary to face down a formidable foe like Wal-Mart. Some feel the problem is the UFCW's old-fashioned, top-down, undemocratic style—a reluctance to develop leadership among rank-and-file workers.

Mike Leonard, the former head of Strategic Programs for the UFCW, who retired in late 2003, says of such critics, "There are a lot of gurus in the labor movement, people who think they have all the answers. . . . They don't know how hard it is to organize Wal-Mart." Leonard says it would be impossible for one union to effectively organize Wal-Mart and still serve members who work for other companies. He has a point. Still, the criticisms have some validity. None of the workers or former workers involved in the organizing effort and interviewed for this book expressed a real sense of ownership of the Wal-Mart campaign. Even a natural leader like Gretchen Adams says she goes wherever the union officials, based in Washington, D.C., ask her to go. It is clear that she has little influence on the campaign's direction. The union consistently fails to use workers' expertise. The UFCW hired Linda Gruen, who worked for Wal-Mart in Las Vegas for six years and was very active in the campaign there, to organize, amazingly, workers at a company other than Wal-Mart, rather than use her years of Wal-Mart expertise to organize her former employer. She refers to the UFCW leadership as the "powers that be."

Conversely, Micki Earwood, an original *Dukes* plaintiff who is articulate, outgoing, and furious with Wal-Mart,

lasted just six weeks working for the UFCW: the union assigned her to organize the very same store from which she'd
just been fired, where management had been running a
smear campaign against her because she'd complained about
discrimination. When she was handing out union leaflets in
the parking lot, management sent her former friends and
coworkers out to taunt and harass her. "People say I'm brave
for being part of the lawsuit," Earwood says, but she thinks
working for the union takes far more guts. Earwood calls organizing "the hardest thing I've ever tried to do," and is
pretty sure she'll never try it again.

The California supermarket strike raised further questions
about the UFCW's effectiveness. Though labor organizers in
the region say the dispute could have been anticipated years
ago, the workers were clearly not prepared for it; they had no
idea how long they'd be on strike and many hadn't saved
enough money to get by. And despite the fact that the entire
labor movement was concerned about how a defeat might affect unionized workers everywhere, the UFCW did not make
effective use of other unions, even rejecting offers of help
from the leadership of the Service Employees International
Union, which has conducted numerous successful strikes in
the region. The grocery workers' disastrous defeat confirmed
the fears of many labor leaders that the UFCW may not be
up to the formidable job of organizing Wal-Mart, at least not
by itself. As of spring 2004, major labor unions are restructuring themselves: the Hotel Employees and Restaurant Employees has merged with UNITE (Union of Needletrades,
Industrial and Textile Employees), which has been organizing

retail workers at H&M and other chain stores. There is serious talk among union insiders of creating a new large-scale labor organization that will do nothing but organize Wal-Mart. Meetings have been held at AFL-CIO headquarters to discuss how the major labor unions might work together on the Wal-Mart challenge. John Wilhelm, president of the Hotel Employees and Restaurant Employees International, has said that organizing Wal-Mart should be labor's highest priority after the November 2004 elections.

Asked how long it will take to unionize Wal-Mart, Gretchen Adams, who is 57, answers without hesitation, "The rest of my life." But she is determined. Recalling her time in Las Vegas, when she couldn't hire experienced, skilled workers because they might be union members, she deadpans, "I'm trying to get Wal-Mart the help it needs."

7

"ATTENTION, SHOPPERS!"

"WAL-MART WOMEN" are not just the cashiers and greeters—they're also the shoppers buying their groceries and kids' school clothes at their local Supercenter. Wal-Mart has been phenomenally successful with women: four out of ten American women visit one of Wal-Mart's stores weekly.[1] They like the low prices, convenience, and overall ease of the shopping experience. Even snobbish elites are discovering its delights: the *New York Times* fashion writer Cathy Horyn recently revealed, to the astonishment of her fellow urban fashionistas, that much of her wardrobe comes from Wal-Mart (the headline read: "Marc Jacobs?" "No, It's Wal-Mart"). Even Paris Hilton famously pledged her allegiance to Wal-Mart after she discovered that it sold more than wallpaper. "I didn't realize it has everything," she enthused. "You can get anything you want there for really, really cheap." Wendy Liebmann, a retail consultant, ecstatically dubs Wal-Mart the "benchmark by which American women rate all shopping."[2]

If only $15 runway knockoffs were Wal-Mart's primary contribution to women's lives. As the nation's largest employer, it has brought American women discrimination, disrespect, low wages, and lousy health plans. But as a shopping destination, it's made them happy.

Joanne Yaccatto is a Canadian market researcher whose work is dedicated to the commercial side of Freud's classic question: "What does a woman want?" She believes women are socially conscious shoppers. Still, in a study she completed in 2003, Yaccatto found that Canadian women named Wal-Mart their "favorite company." The findings were consistent with her usual advice to retailers: "Do anything and everything to make women's lives simpler."[3] Women work outside the home far more than in the past, and still do twice as much housework and child care as men.[4] On top of that, they are also responsible for most of the family shopping, and make 80 percent of all consumer purchases.[5] They are badly in need of ways to make that task easier.

In one of Wal-Mart's many commercials aimed at women, a school guidance counselor is shown helping kids at work, then rushing home to tend to her own children. She confides to the viewer the difficulties of supporting a family on her modest public servant's salary. How does she cope with so many demands on her budget and time? By shopping at Wal-Mart, of course. "Listen to your guidance counselor," a kindly sounding voice-over concludes.

Wal-Mart knows how badly women need convenience. Customers love its low prices, not to mention the "one-stop shopping" it offers. At a Wal-Mart 24-hour Supercenter, you can change a tire, buy groceries for dinner, and get a new pair of shoes and some yard furniture—a set of errands that once would have required a long afternoon of visits to far-flung merchants. The underpaid, overworked American woman delights in spending as little as possible, all in one place.

LouAnn Lofton, writing for *The Motley Fool,* a newsletter of investment advice, explains why the Wal-Mart Superstore is such a threat to other supermarkets:

> One truly must experience a Supercenter firsthand to understand the draw. When I lived in Memphis, Tenn., a few years ago, I did every bit of my grocery shopping across the Mississippi River. The Wal-Mart Supercenter in West Memphis, Ark., was my home away from home. The convenience of buying absolutely anything I wanted, cheaply and in one store, more than made up for the few extra minutes of driving. . . . I loved shopping there, and miss it still.[6]

There are, of course, aspects to this shopping bliss that both men and women enjoy, but there is no doubt that Wal-Mart is particularly attuned to women. In a 1999 study of female consumers conducted for *Women's Wear Daily* by the market research company International Communication Research, respondents described perfectly what Wal-Mart has known for years.[7] They wanted a bargain, and they wanted it quickly. Nearly 40 percent of the respondents named price as their most important consideration. And as Wal-Mart—an unadorned eyesore surrounded by a parking lot, even its logo aggressively devoid of flourish—has known all along, if you want to woo the ladies, looks don't matter: only 2.5 percent of the respondents to the *Women's Wear Daily* survey felt a store's appearance was a factor likely to influence their shopping.

The delightful weekend boutique hopping depicted on *Sex and the City* is, alas, a fantasy. Few real-life women can afford to take pleasure in shopping without making a fetish of intensely practical concerns: when *Women's Wear Daily*'s researchers asked women what they enjoyed most about shopping, "getting a bargain" rated highest. Leisurely, sociable shopping appears to be a luxury only Paris Hilton can afford. Most of the women surveyed did not want to spend much time shopping, and didn't. Across all age groups, the study found, the American woman spends less than two hours on a typical shopping expedition, and the lower her income, the less time she spends.

In a finding particularly distressing to the fashion industry, *Women's Wear Daily* found that women didn't much care about keeping up with the hottest trends. They are increasingly indifferent to fashion: 58 percent said they now care less about it than they did five years ago. Surprisingly, young women (18–34) were even more likely to be losing interest in fashion than older women. Wal-Mart has been wise to this apathy for years. Although, as *The New York Times* fashion writer Cathy Moryn noted, Wal-Mart has become trendier in recent years, it still looks dowdy compared to its fellow discounter Target.

By making itself just stylish enough to compete with popular down-market mall brands, Wal-Mart has benefited from, and perhaps encouraged, young women's declining interest

in trends. In July 2002, Wal-Mart landed exclusive rights to
the teen clothing line bearing the names of the celebrity
twins Mary-Kate and Ashley Olsen, the teen actress-de-
signer duo, and a walking and talking brand. Child stars who
began their careers as infants on the popular TV sitcom *Full
House* in the early 1990s, the twins now lend their name to,
and preside over, a vast empire of products, including dolls,
a cartoon, books, a video game, sheets, a fragrance—and
clothes and accessories sold at Wal-Mart. This line, "mary-
kateandashley," has been enormously successful, making
over $750 million in 2002. Wal-Mart is creating 600-square-
foot boutiques within some of its stores, the better to display all the Olsen merchandise.[8] The Olsen twins' appeal is
much like that of Sam Walton. As Mary-Kate and Ashley say
in nearly every interview, "We're just normal kids, except
we. . . run a company." Tapping into the popularity of these
bland teens, described by Wal-Mart CEO Lee Scott as "fashion magnets,"[9] demonstrates that Wal-Mart brilliantly understands not only overworked middle-aged women, but also
their daughters who, after all, do plenty of shopping. In
2000, teenagers spent $155 billion on clothing, makeup,
CDs, and other "discretionary" purchases.[10]

American women also appreciate Wal-Mart's accommo-
dation to their increasing girth. The shopping setback that
Women's Wear Daily's poll respondents rated most irksome
was being unable to find their size. According to the Centers
for Disease Control, in 1999–2000, 62 percent of American
women over the age of 20 were overweight, up from 51.2

percent for the last time period surveyed, 1988–1994.[11] More than half of American women are a size 12 or larger, and in 2001, American women spent $17.1 billion on plus-size clothing, 19 percent of all the dollars spent on women's apparel, and 22 percent more than in 2000.[12] Plus-size is the fastest-growing category in women's clothing.

As even some of its feminist foes acknowledge, Wal-Mart is one of the retailers most attentive to the big woman's needs. In February 2003, the company began carrying its teen brands—mary-kateandashley and Faded Glory Jeans—in a brand it calls Girlswear Plus sizes in 1,300 stores. Zaftig girls can now buy peasant tops, low-rise Capri pants, and other trendy items at Wal-Mart, advertised by the appealing girl-power slogan "Real Sizes for Real Girls." "Whoah baby!" enthused Michele Weston, a columnist for Venus Divas, a fashion website for large women, "This is a revolution."[13]

Seventy percent of heavy women say they prefer the term "curvaceous" to "plus-size," according to a study released in May 2003 by Leflein Associates, a market research firm. But Wal-Mart didn't need to be told: the company was, by that time, already the exclusive retailer for Curvation, a lingerie line for large ladies whose spokesmodel is the stunning rapper and actress Queen Latifah (she is also a spokesmodel for Lane Bryant, a chain that sells only plus-sized clothing). "I look like America," she recently boasted.[14] In an interview published on a fashion website, Queen Latifah enthused, "I am proud to be a curvaceous woman and represent a brand like Curvation that embodies the strong spirit of sexy, curvaceous women everywhere."[15] Wal-Mart knows that the voluptuous don't just want clothes that fit: like most women, they want to look seductive.

Of course, Wal-Mart's enlightened approach to the female body has much to do with its long-time customer base: the have-nots, who are even more likely than the rest of America to be fat. Regardless of race or ethnicity, low-income women—defined, in this context, as those living on incomes below 130 percent of the federal poverty line—are about 50 percent more likely to be obese than women of higher economic status.[16]

Like Wal-Mart's female worker, its customer is overwhelmingly poor and working-class. One study of the supermarket industry found that 34 percent of Wal-Mart customers said they were just "getting by" economically (29 percent described themselves as "comfortable").[17] Wal-Mart benefits from the economic pressures faced by so many American women, as both consumers and workers. Of course, by discriminating against women and paying them so badly, Wal-Mart only worsens those pressures. The working poor are even more likely than other Americans to shop at Wal-Mart, not necessarily because they find it a shopper's paradise—though, of course, some do—but because they need the discounts, or live in remote areas with few other options. Through shoppers as well as "associates," Wal-Mart is making billions from female poverty.

Betty Dukes has noted that Wal-Mart takes out ads in her local paper the same day the community's poorest citizens collect their welfare checks. "They are promoting themselves to low-income people," she says. "That's who they lure. They don't lure the rich. . . . They understand the economy of America. They know the haves and have-nots. They don't put Wal-Mart in Piedmonts. They don't put Wal-Mart in those high-end parts of the community. They plant themselves right in the middle of Poorville."

Dukes is right that Wal-Mart does much more business in poor areas than in rich ones. A 2001 study by Andrew Franklin, an economist at Iowa State University, showed that Wal-Mart operated "primarily" in poor and working-class communities, finding, in the bone-dry language of his discipline, "a significant negative relationship between median household income and Wal-Mart's presence in the market."[18] Although fancy retailers noted with chagrin during the 2001 recession, that absolutely everybody shops at Wal-Mart— "Even people with $100,000 incomes shop at Wal-Mart," a PR flack for one upscale mall fumed[19]—the Bloomingdale's set is not the discounter's primary market, and probably never will be. Recession hysteria aside, Neiman Marcus and Godiva have nothing to fear: only 6 percent of Wal-Mart shoppers have annual incomes of more than $100,000. A 2003 study found that 28 percent of Wal-Mart Supercenter customers lived on incomes of less than $25,000 a year.[20] More than 95 percent of white Americans have bank accounts, and not having one has long been considered a sign of dire poverty. More than 20 percent of Wal-Mart shoppers have no bank account.[21] Almost half of Wal-Mart Supercenter customers are blue-collar workers and their families, and 20 percent are unemployed or elderly.[22]

Al Zack, who until his retirement in 2004 was the United Food and Commercial Workers' vice president for Strategic Programs, observes that appealing to the poor was "Sam Walton's real genius. He figured out how to make money off poverty. He located his first stores in poor rural areas and discovered a real market. The only problem with this business model is, it needs more poverty to grow." That problem is cleverly solved by creating more bad jobs worldwide. In a chilling reversal of Henry Ford's strategy, which was to pay his workers amply so they could buy Ford cars, Wal-Mart's stinginess contributes to an economy in which, increasingly, workers can only afford to shop at Wal-Mart.

Many of the speeches at Wal-Mart's 2003 annual meeting focused on the company's concern for its low-income female consumer and its dedication to making her life easier. "We are improving standards of living" through low prices, company officials emphasized. CEO Lee Scott told a story about a reporter who was "from a big city," like many critics who "don't understand Wal-Mart." Having written some critical news stories about the company, she went late one Saturday night, on Easter weekend, to her local Wal-Mart, where she encountered "a very tired mother" buying new clothes for her children. The customer explained, "Without Wal-Mart I could not afford to have my girls in new Easter dresses and shoes tomorrow. Now I can take pride in my girls." The audience at the meeting, mostly Wal-Mart workers and managers, was visibly moved by this story, deeply believing that they were part of a company helping people just like them.

Workers sometimes complain about rude customers, but most genuinely enjoy the customers—perhaps surprisingly, given the difficulties of being cheerful on one's feet all day. Many are aware that the customers' circumstances are similar to their own. They identify with the shopper, understanding her poverty, her time crunch, her kids' needs—and her weight problems.

One long-time department manager in Ohio cheerfully recalls her successful job interview at Wal-Mart. Because of her weight, she told her interviewers she'd be better able to help the customer. "I told them I wanted to work in the ladies department because I'm a heavy girl." She understands the frustrations of the large shopper, she told them: "'You know, you go into Lane Bryant and some skinny girl is trying to sell you clothes.' They laughed at that and said, 'You get a second interview!'"

Like this worker, most of the Wal-Mart women interviewed for this book feel a kind of solidarity with the shoppers. *Dukes* plaintiff Cleo Page, who no longer works at Wal-Mart, says she was a great customer service manager because she understood the customers: "I knew how people feel when they shop, so I was really empathetic."

Many Wal-Mart workers say they began working at their local Wal-Mart because they shopped there; when they needed a job, they filled out its application because Wal-Mart was already such a familiar part of their lives. "I was practically born in Wal-Mart," says Alyssa Warrick, a former Wal-Mart worker now attending Truman State University in Kirksville, Missouri. "My mom is obsessed with shopping. . . . I thought it would be pretty easy since I knew where most of the stuff was." Most assumed they would love working at Wal-Mart because they were dedicated customers. "I always loved shopping there," enthuses *Dukes* plaintiff Dee Gunter, "That's why I wanted to work for 'em."

Shopping is traditionally a world of intense female communication and bonding, and the identification between clerk and shopper has long been part of the reason that women have excelled in retail sales. Page, who still shops at Wal-Mart, is now a lingerie saleswoman at Mervyn's (owned by Target). "I do enjoy retail," she says. "I like feeling needed and I like helping people, especially women." She likes her department because women "need help with something that's kind of intimate. Girdles and bras and all that stuff. . . we talk about liposuction a lot. We laugh about stuff. . . . One woman was, like, 'Why do they make workout bras that you can see through to the skin?' We say, 'Who do you think made that?'" She laughs. "A man."

Dukes says, "I strive to give Wal-Mart customers one hundred percent of my abilities." This sentiment was repeated by numerous other Wal-Mart workers, always with heartfelt sincerity. Betty Hamilton, a 61-year-old clerk in a Las Vegas Sam's Club, won her club's customer service award last year. She is very knowledgeable about jewelry, her favorite department, and proud of it. "I am jewelry," she says. "I love it. It is so interesting and fascinating and fun." Hamilton resents her employer—she complains about sexual harassment and discrimination, and feels she has been penalized on the job for her union sympathies—but remains deeply devoted to her customers. She enjoys imparting her knowledge to shoppers so "they can walk out of there and feel like they know something." Like Page, Hamilton feels she is helping people. "It makes me so happy when I sell something that I know is an extraordinarily good buy," she says. "I feel like I've done somebody a really good favor."

The enthusiasm of these women for their jobs, despite the workplace indignities many of them have faced, should not assure anybody that the company's abuses don't matter. In fact, it should underscore the tremendous debt Wal-Mart owes women: this company has built its vast profits not only on women's drudgery, but also on their joy, creativity, and genuine care for the customer.

Will consumers return that solidarity, and punish Wal-Mart for discriminating against women? Do customers care about workers as much as workers care about them? Unions and women's groups are hoping they do, and believe that the common ground between Wal-Mart's workers and shoppers can be politicized.

The National Organization for Women, inspired by *Dukes v. Wal-Mart,* has been attempting to educate female consumers about the situation faced by the female Wal-Mart worker. In June 2002, NOW, naming Wal-Mart its fifth "Merchant of Shame," launched a public education campaign against the retailer, letting the public know that Wal-Mart discriminates against its female workers. "It's part of our emphasis on economic justice. We don't think Wal-Mart is a woman-friendly workplace," says Olga Vives, NOW's vice president for action. NOW has asked Wal-Mart for a meeting to discuss its complaints, but since the company has not responded, Vives says, "We are getting their attention in other ways." On September 28, 2002, a crisp and sunny fall day, members from 600 NOW chapters demonstrated at Wal-Mart stores across the country, from Tallahassee to Salt Lake City. At the Wal-Mart in Alexandria, Virginia, a small but spirited crowd of about 40 protesters—a mix of suburban soccer moms, activists from the city, and burly (male) union members—picketed and chanted on the sidewalk, staying out of the parking lot to avoid arrest.

At the time, Bill Wertz, a Wal-Mart spokesman, told me that, since NOW's protests were based on a lawsuit whose charges hadn't been proved in court, the company had no comment. Since then, other Wal-Mart spokespeople have made similar statements about the NOW campaign.

As *Dukes* moved through the discovery process, the United Food and Commercial Workers Union (UFCW) enthusiastically joined NOW's effort to reach the female consumer. Susan Phillips, a UFCW vice president and treasurer who is also head of the union's Working Women's Department, began saying in frequent speeches to female labor audiences, "As women, we have tremendous power. We control both sides of the cash register. We are the cashiers on one side and we are the customers on the other side. If we join hands across the cash register, we can change the economic future for women in America."

At a November 18, 2002, press conference in Washington, D.C., NOW and UFCW leaders announced a UFCW-initiated

National Day of Action on November 21, and rallies were held in more than 100 cities and towns, supported by a broad coalition of religious, environmental, student, and labor groups. At the press conference, Gretchen Adams, the former Wal-Mart comanager and *Dukes* witness who is now working for the union, took the podium with confidence and gave a stirring speech; a couple days later, she flew to Louisville, Kentucky, to address a National Day of Action rally there.

NOW urges the public not to shop at Wal-Mart. The UFCW has been avoiding boycott talk in most places but is pressing for local actions, and Doug Dority, president of the UFCW, announced at the press conference that the union was "calling for a boycott in Las Vegas"—where a vigorous organizing campaign was already under way. Wal-Mart has committed numerous violations of the right to organize, but because it is such a heavily organized city, the union enjoys broad community support. Elsewhere, however, the UFCW is not ready to take that step. "It's hard to boycott and organize at the same time," says Dority, "Because Wal-Mart uses that against you [telling workers]: 'Hey, the union is trying to take away your job.'"

Boycott campaigns definitely do alienate some workers. Dee Gunter was angry when told that NOW was encouraging people not to shop at Wal-Mart. "You're not hurting Wal-Mart when you do that," she said. "You're hurting that woman who's working there and trying to get by, because you're threatening her job. You can't hold the people responsible for what corporate's doing." Gunter wasn't the only worker who felt that way, which is understandable, given employees' intense identification with the company.

NOW leaders still urge customers to shop elsewhere but, partly with this problem in mind, in May 2003, the organization launched its Adopt-a-Store campaign, an ongoing attempt to communicate more directly with workers as well as shoppers. NOW members nationwide go into local Wal-Mart stores, wearing buttons displaying the message "Wal-Mart: Always Discriminates"—a play on Wal-Mart's own slogan "Wal-Mart: Always Low Prices," which employees wear on badges. The NOW button "has a little smiley-face, it's really cute—a smiley-face that's frowning!" says NOW's Vives with a laugh. The frowny-face is a play on Wal-Mart's own ubiquitous smiley-face. In contrast to the demonstrations and pickets that NOW organized earlier, Vives calls the campaign "a more direct action. It's more aggressive and it puts more pressure on the company. It also provides Wal-Mart workers with more visible support."

In the stores, NOW activists also distribute palm-sized cards with the question "Wal-Mart: *Always* Low Prices, But Who Pays?" On the back, the card gives information about the lawsuit and urges customers to "talk to your Wal-Mart's store manager and ask for an end to unfair discrimination against women."

At least 500 or 600 activists, representing 20 NOW chapters, have participated in the Adopt-a-Store campaign. Many of those are in California, where the lawsuit has received greater press attention than elsewhere in the country because it is in a San Francisco federal court and the current plaintiffs are from California. Chapters in Boise, Idaho; Springfield, Missouri; Philadelphia; and Nassau County, New York, have also adopted stores.

In an undeniably more glamorous development, a former Miss America, Carolyn Sapp, inspired by a *Business Week* article about the *Dukes* lawsuit, has started an organization called Women Versus Wal-Mart, through which she also hopes to educate consumers.[23] Sapp, who wore the Miss America tiara in 1992, has an upbeat and gregarious manner befitting a highly successful beauty queen. But she has had quite sobering experiences. Almost killed by an abusive boyfriend more than a decade ago, she has long been outspoken against domestic violence, and founded a public education organization called Safe Places (of which her new anti-Wal-Mart project is a subsidiary). Violence against women is, Sapp says, "an ugly issue," hardly the bland noncontroversial stuff Miss America is expected to speak about, like child literacy and finding cures for diseases. Reading about Wal-Mart, she realized that the experiences of women like Dukes were very much like her own. "These women are not being physically abused," she says, "but they're being emotionally abused and economically abused. And I was outraged, because we all shop at Wal-Mart."

Since then, Sapp has founded Women Versus Wal-Mart and participated in numerous rallies calling for Wal-Mart to treat female employees with fairness. In one of these, organized by workers in Las Vegas, she and a number of women, some of them *Dukes* witnesses, wore Miss America–style tiaras sporting sashes bearing the message "Women Versus Wal-Mart." Sapp travels the country speaking to local groups who are trying to keep Wal-Mart out of their towns. Many of these organizations are now adding sex discrimination to their long list of complaints about the retailer, which include low wages, ugly sprawl, traffic, and outrageous tax breaks, among others.

"I think when women realize how Wal-Mart is treating other women, they're going to stop shopping at Wal-Mart," says Sapp. She encourages people to ask themselves, "'Do I really want to support this type of free enterprise?' Because it's not free for these women."

Of course, Wal-Mart is associated in many women's minds with female celebrities of wholesome reputation. Kathie Lee Gifford used to have an exclusive clothing line with the company (which caused her great embarrassment when the garments turned out to be made by underpaid Honduran children). Wal-Mart's annual meetings have frequently attracted major celebrities, including a beaming Halle Berry at the 2004 meeting. Perhaps it's a sign of the declining importance of Miss America in our national culture that Sapp isn't as famous as Kathie Lee, Berry, Queen Latifah, or the Olsen sisters. Nevertheless, she lends the cause of Wal-Mart's women a clean-cut, mainstream cachet.

Market research suggests that women do care about a corporation's behavior toward women, and that what they hear about a company can influence their buying habits. In one of her studies, Joanne Yaccatto (author of *The 80% Minority*) found that 75 percent of women said that, to get and keep their business, a company had to care about the community, and about its employees, particularly female workers. Women,

she writes, want to do business with "a place where women
are part of the company hierarchy—from the mailroom to
the executives suites. They care about how the company treats
women." Yaccatto feels strongly that when women learn more
about sex discrimination at Wal-Mart, the company's profits
could suffer. "With Wal-Mart having a class-action suit against
it, they stand at great risk of alienating their greatest consumer
constituency," she says. She felt that *Dukes* was "not yet in the
collective consciousness" but that when women learned about
it, Wal-Mart could face trouble. NOW president Kim Gandy
agrees, vowing, "Wal-Mart should know that continuing their
greedy, abusive ways will cost them the business of thinking
consumers."

The optimistic conviction of feminists like Gandy, that female consumers will turn against Wal-Mart in large numbers,
is encouraging, but difficult to share. None of these feminist
consumer campaigns have so far had any discernible effect on
the company's sales. Public education focused on Wal-Mart
customers is crucial, because losing sales is one of the few
things Wal-Mart truly fears, but without much broader efforts
to change the political context in which the company operates,
they may be doomed to failure—because Wal-Mart's prices
are so low. The company effectively pits poor women against
other poor women. As April Hotchkiss, the sales associate in
Pueblo, Colorado, sometimes tells customers, "You're bene-
fiting from me getting screwed. Thanks for shopping at Wal-
Mart!" She laughs, "Hey, I try to be positive."

Many women welcome the new Wal-Marts opening in
their communities, despite the company's growing reputation

for low wages and sex discrimination. The *Winona* (Minnesota) *Post* extensively covered a controversy over whether to allow a Wal-Mart Supercenter into the small town; the letters to the editor in response offer a window into the female customer's loyalty to Wal-Mart. Though the paper devoted substantial space to the sex discrimination case, many female readers vehemently defended the retailer. From the nearby town of Rollingstone, Cindy Kay wrote that she needed the new Wal-Mart because the local stores didn't carry large enough sizes. She denounced the local anti-Wal-Mart campaign as a plot by rich and thin elites: "I'm glad those people can fit into their clothes and can afford to shop [elsewhere]."[24] A week later, Carolyn Goree, a preschool teacher also hoping for a Winona Wal-Mart, wrote in a letter to the *Post* editor that when she shops at most stores, $200 fills only a bag or two, but at Wal-Mart "I come out with a cart full top and bottom. How good that feels." Lacking a local Wal-Mart, Goree drives over the Wisconsin border to get her fix. She was incensed by an earlier letter writer's lament that some workers make only $15,000 yearly. "Come on!" Goree objected, "Is $15,000 that bad of a yearly income? I'm a single mom and when working out of my home, I made $12,000 tops and that was with child support. I too work, pay for a mortgage, lights, food, everything to live. Everything in life is a choice.... I am for the little man/woman—I'm one of them. So I say stand up and get a Wal-Mart."[25]

Sara Jennings, a Winona reader living on disability payments that total $8,000, heartily concurred. After paying her rent, phone, electric, and cable bills, Jennings can barely afford to treat herself to McDonald's. Of a recent trip to the LaCrosse, Wisconsin, Wal-Mart, she raved, "Oh boy, what a great treat. Lower prices and good quality clothes to choose from. It was like heaven for me." She, too, strongly defended the workers' $15,000 yearly income: "Boy, now that is a lot of money. I could live with that." She closed with a plea to the readers: "I'm sure you all make a lot more money than I. And I'm sure I speak for a lot of seniors and very low-income people. We need this Wal-Mart. There is nothing downtown."[26]

A customer saves 17–39 percent by buying groceries at Wal-Mart rather than from a competitor, according to retail analysts.[27] Wal-Mart offers such low prices that people will shop there even if they are aware of the company's crimes. The UFCW's Susan Phillips admits, "We can't even get our members not to shop at Wal-Mart."

Betty Dukes heartily approves of the women's groups who are encouraging the public not to shop at Wal-Mart. "You have to be radical," she says. "You have to be aggressive to create change." But she wonders if a boycott will work, given customers' poverty, and she empathizes with those who have to shop at the store. "A lot of people in my community, Pittsburg, are low-income, minority, poor." Imagining a typical Pittsburg woman, Dukes says, "Suppose I don't want to go to Wal-Mart because I'm sympathetic to the issues, but my baby needs milk." Prices at Safeway, she points out, are much higher than at Wal-Mart. "Sometimes you can't be all that you would like to be," she says, meaning that the poor can't always afford the luxury of being socially conscious consumers, "And Wal-Mart knows that." Admits

Joaquin Ross, a publicist for Women Versus Wal-Mart, "We may never convince lower-income families to shop elsewhere, because Wal-Mart does undercut a lot of the more responsible corporations."

Most of the "more responsible" corporations have richer consumers, who have more retail options and may thus be freer to shop their consciences. The Target shopper—also female—has a median income of $54,000.[28] Half of Target shoppers are college graduates, and more than half have managerial or professional jobs. Market research has also shown that unionized grocery stores like Safeway, Albertson's, and Kroger attract higher-income shoppers than Wal-Mart does.[29]

Some activists have negotiated this problem by finding creative alternatives to the boycott. Far from telling consumers not to shop at the "Big Box," on the November 2002 National Day of Action, many UFCW locals dramatized consumer power through "shop-ins," urging protesters to go into the store, buy something while wearing a T-shirt with the UFCW's phone number on it, and tell employees they supported their right to join a union. In Seekonk, Massachusetts, a UFCW local even gave each November 21 protester a $20 bill to spend at Wal-Mart, donating the purchases to a nearby women's shelter. The Coalition of Labor Union Women (CLUW), which includes 20,000 women from 60 unions, has embraced this tactic and continued to organize shop-ins in Kansas City, Missouri, Cincinnati, upstate New York, and elsewhere.

"Attention, Shoppers . . ." reads a CLUW flyer distributed to women shopping in a Canonsburg, Pennsylvania, Wal-Mart:

Wal-Mart Workers Need a Voice!

As a working woman, you know how hard it is to make ends meet.

We know, too. Like you, we are working women.

So are the women who work inside this Wal-Mart store.

The flyer went on to explain the pay inequities uncovered by the *Dukes* case, interjecting succinct commentary ("This is no way for the world's largest employer to behave!") and urging customers to "Support Wal-Mart workers by letting the managers in this store know what you think about Wal-Mart's unequal pay for women."

Another obstacle to achieving progressive goals through consumer pressure on Wal-Mart is the politics of many Wal-Mart shoppers. Obviously Wal-Mart did not become the most profitable company in the world by appealing only to conservative fanatics, but it is clear that Wal-Mart's traditional customers are far more easily mobilized by right-wing Christian organizations than by feminists (some of that may change as Wal-Mart moves into more coastal and urban markets). The company attracted controversy and criticism in May 2003, when it decided, in response to complaints from (mostly female) customers, not to stock the boisterous men's magazines *FHM, Maxim,* and *Stuff.* The customers had been galvanized, as the national media mostly did not report, by national Christian organizations. Although Wal-Mart framed this as a sudden decision based on a few complaints, it was the result of years of campaigning by the right, who were easily able to organize customers to complain. (*Playboy,* which had never been available at Wal-Mart, immediately responded by gleefully ribbing the retailer, calling for Wal-Mart's female employees, its "sexiest assets," to take off their smocks and "put on a happy face for *Playboy*'s cameras.")

It might seem odd that a company that would force female managers to hang out at strip clubs—and has a long record of ignoring cretinous, knuckle-dragging harassment—should get so prim and proper about mildly racy magazines. But it's perfectly logical economics: unlike its female workforce, the women who shop at Wal-Mart can't be ignored, and many of them have conservative values.

In a similar response to fundamentalist Christian pressure, Wal-Mart, the nation's top seller of music, doesn't sell CDs bearing parental-advisory labels, and carries sanitized versions of many CDs, or sells them with less offensive covers. In June 2003, just on the heels of the Christian victory over *Maxim*, in response to another organized campaign by a coalition that included Concerned Women for America, the American Family Association, and many other conservative groups with grassroots networks of Wal-Mart shoppers, Wal-Mart agreed to conceal salacious *Cosmopolitan* magazine headlines ("Blow His Mind!" "What He's Thinking About You. . . NAKED") from checkout line bystanders, inventing a new kind of magazine rack that shows the magazine's titles, but conceals models' cleavage and racy promises of "Secret Sex Tips." Explaining its decision, Wal-Mart again cited feedback from "customers," without mentioning the organizations behind the campaign.

This does suggest that there is some hope in consumer pressure strategies, but the challenges feminists face here are

formidable. Where the fundamentalist Christians only demand changes in Wal-Mart's merchandise or its presentation,
NOW and the unions demand broad reform of its labor
practices, which is a taller order and far more threatening to
the company's profits. Also, as one Christian activist, a Mo-
bile, Alabama, mother, said of her personal success lobbying
her local Wal-Mart to cover up *Cosmo,* "there is strength in
numbers."[30] Wal-Mart is more afraid of the Christian right
than of NOW because organized feminism's base doesn't
shop at Wal-Mart, while the Christian Right's does. (To the
extent that NOW sympathizers do shop at Wal-Mart, there
is little evidence that they base their consumer decisions on
their beliefs.) Ads for Christian country music frequently
conclude with, "Available at Wal-Mart," and in the days before *Glorious Appearing,* Tim LaHaye's best-selling novel
about the Rapture, hit bookstore shelves, Wal-Mart gave
away the first chapter for free.

Wal-Mart shoppers *are* conservative. Despite some expan-
sion into cities, the women who shop at Wal-Mart still live
mostly in rural areas and exurbs: about 70 percent of Wal-
Mart's Supercenters are outside the top 100 metropolitan
areas. The company prefers regions where unions are weak.
Wal-Mart customers are overwhelmingly Republican, according to Mark Husson, a Merrill Lynch analyst, who found
in a study of the grocery industry that Wal-Mart had a "high
share in Republican markets and low share in Democratic-
controlled markets." Husson pointed out that the influence
of unions in Democratic areas creates a hostile climate for
the retailer to open and operate stores. Safeway and

Kroger—both unionized—draw mostly Democrats, probably because of geography.[31]

Some Wal-Mart customers may, in fact, feel that they are following their conscience by shopping at Wal-Mart. Alyssa Warrick—who was so thoroughly disillusioned by the company
that she created a website depicting Sam Walton as the Anti-
Christ, an unusually irreverent attitude toward a man most employees stubbornly adore—says that in southwestern Missouri,
where she grew up, politics plays a part in customer loyalty to
Wal-Mart. The region has an unusually high density of Wal-
Mart stores—one in nearly every county seat—and is known
for its conservatism. As Warrick points out, Springfield is John
Ashcroft's hometown. Locals associate Wal-Mart with conservative values, and that is one of the many reasons they shop
there. "A lot of people like that Wal-Mart is anti-union," says
Warrick, "I think they think unions are antibusiness."

Of course, many conservatives and fundamentalist Christians support equality for women; most of the current *Dukes*
plaintiffs are ardent worshippers, and Dukes's congregation
passionately supports her cause. Most churches have not been
outspoken on Wal-Mart's sex discrimination, though some,
especially those with liberal or African American congrega-
tions, have joined the UFCW's protests. There are surely many
more Christians who agree with the aims of these coalitions,
even some of the same people who opposed the sex magazines. After all, Dukes is upset that Wal-Mart sells beer, and
was glad to see the men's magazines come off the shelf: "In
the old days," she said disapprovingly, "[Wal-Mart] didn't have
these sexually explicit magazines." If the lawsuit continues to

draw attention and inspire protest, perhaps some surprising alliances will emerge.

It is crucial that Wal-Mart's liberal and progressive critics make use of the growing public indignation at the company, but given the political challenges they face, it is equally crucial to do this in ways that remind people that their power does not stop at their shopping dollars. It is admirable to drive across town and pay more for toilet paper to avoid shopping at Wal-Mart, but such a gesture is, unfortunately, not enough. The Christian Right's efforts to mobilize consumers are successful because participating in them reminds people that they are much more than Wal-Mart shoppers— they are believers in Christ and members of a large social movement wielding significant political power, even though as individuals they may be ordinary working people. As long as people identify themselves as consumers and nothing more, Wal-Mart wins.

The invention of the "consumer" identity has been an important part of a long process of eroding workers' power, and is one reason working people now have so little power against business. According to the social historian Stuart Ewen, in the early years of mass production, the late nineteenth and early twentieth century, modernizing capitalism sought to turn people who thought of themselves primarily as "workers" into "consumers."[32] Business elites wanted people to dream not of satisfying work and egalitarian societies—as many did at that time—but of the beautiful things they could buy with their paychecks. To succeed, mass production required people to consume much more and to consent without rebellion to exploitative conditions at work. This, in Ewen's view, was the agenda of much early advertising: business hoped to create an "individual who could locate his needs and frustrations in terms of the consumption of goods rather than the quality and content of his life (work)."[33] Business was quite successful in this project, which continued throughout the twentieth century. In addition to replacing the "worker," the "consumer" has also effectively displaced the citizen. (It is worth pointing out, though, as Lizabeth Cohen does in *A Consumer's Republic: The Politics of Mass Consumption in Postwar America*, that throughout the twentieth century, these have been fluid and shifting categories, and citizens have often used their consumer power in politically effective ways. For the reasons discussed, however, Wal-Mart is a difficult target for this type of activism.)[34] That's why, when most Americans hear about the Wal-Mart's worker-rights abuses, their first reaction is to feel guilty about shopping there. A tiny minority will respond by shopping elsewhere—and only a handful will take any further action. A worker might call her union and organize a picket. A citizen might write to her congressman or local newspaper, or galvanize her church and knitting circle to visit local management. A consumer makes an isolated, politically slight decision: to shop or not to shop. Most of the time, Wal-Mart has her exactly where it wants her, because the intelligent choice for anyone thinking as a consumer is not to make a political statement, but to seek the best bargain, and the greatest convenience.

The CLUW and the UFCW are targeting the public as workers, arguing that the "low, low prices" are not worth it when Wal-Mart is lowering standards for wages and benefits nationwide for all workers. That may be a promising approach. But to effectively battle corporate criminals like Wal-Mart, the public also must be engaged as citizens, not merely as shoppers and workers. What kind of politics could do that? Unlike so many horrible things, Wal-Mart cannot be blamed on George W. Bush. The Arkansas-based company prospered under the state's native son Bill Clinton when he was governor and president. Sam Walton and his wife, Helen, were close friends with the Clintons, and for several years, Hillary Clinton, whose corporate law firm represented Wal-Mart, served on the company's board of directors. Bill Clinton's "welfare reform" has provided Wal-Mart with a ready workforce of women who have no choice but to accept the company's poverty wages and discriminatory policies.

Still, George W. Bush has most certainly been good for Wal-Mart, too. Retailers like to make campaign contributions to Republicans, partly because Republicans tend to oppose raising the minimum wage. But even compared to other large retail companies, Wal-Mart's political contributions lean significantly to the right—85 percent of the company's 2004 political contributions went to Republicans—and with good reason. Republicans are much more likely to support efforts by corporate lobbyists to weaken labor protections, including, for example, attempts to weaken and limit class-action suits and overtime laws, which would be favored by Wal-Mart for obvious reasons. Republican appointees to the National Labor Relations Board (NLRB) are also far less sympathetic to workers and to unions.

The good news is that Wal-Mart has drawn more criticism under Bush than under Clinton. Both the public and the business media are more inclined to criticize big business in a sluggish economy. *Dukes* has attracted a light but constant flurry of media coverage. Headlines in major newspapers have asked "Is Wal-Mart Bad for America?" The public has expressed increasing concern about the fact that most of Wal-Mart's goods are made in China by women who work in sweatshop conditions and that, closer to home, women like Dukes face discrimination—shameful in a twenty-first-century company. Anti-Wal-Mart stories appeared in the papers nearly every day of 2003, most of them deserved.

In this climate, a handful of Democratic politicians have been standing up to the retailer. California Assemblywoman Sally Lieber, who represents the 22nd Assembly District and is a former mayor of Mountain View, was outraged when she learned about the sex discrimination charges in *Dukes v. Wal-Mart*; she smelled blood when, tipped off by dissatisfied workers, her office discovered that Wal-Mart was encouraging its workers to apply for public assistance, "in the middle of the worst state budget crisis in history!" California had a $38 billion deficit at the time, and Lieber was enraged that taxpayers would be subsidizing Wal-Mart's low wages, bringing new meaning to the term "corporate welfare."

Lieber was angry, too, that Wal-Mart's welfare dependence made it nearly impossible for responsible employers to compete with the retail giant. It was as if taxpayers were unknowingly funding a massive plunge to the bottom in wages and benefits—quite possibly their own. She teamed up with anti-Wal-Mart beauty queen Carolyn Sapp, and the two held a press conference on July 23, 2003, to expose Wal-Mart's welfare scam. The Wal-Mart documents—instructions explaining how to apply for Food Stamps, Medi-Cal (the state's health-care assistance program), and forms of welfare—were blown up on posterboard and displayed at the press conference. NOW, 9 to 5, and the Coalition for Equal Pay sent representatives, all making the point that Wal-Mart's low wages were a women's issue and pointing to the *Dukes* suit as evidence of the company's systemic discrimination against women. (The morning of the press conference, a Wal-Mart worker who wouldn't give her name for fear of being fired snuck into Lieber's office. "I just wanted to say, right on!" she told the assemblywoman.) California NOW was already staging protests at Wal-Mart stores in San Leandro and elsewhere, to call attention to a scheduled hearing in the *Dukes* case. (The class-certification hearing was scheduled to take place that day, but it was postponed until September because the intensely thorough discovery process had generated such a massive pile of documents that the judge was unable to read through it in time.) If women were not being discriminated against, these advocates argued, many would earn enough to stay off welfare.

Wal-Mart spokespeople have denied that the company encourages employees to collect public assistance, but the documents speak for themselves. They bear the Wal-Mart logo, and one is labeled "Wal-Mart: Instructions for Associates." Both documents instruct employees in procedures for applying to "Social Service Agencies." Most Wal-Mart workers interviewed for this book had coworkers who worked full-time for the company and received public assistance, and some had been in that situation themselves. In the past, company spokespeople have acknowledged that some employees depend on government programs for health insurance. Public welfare is very clearly part of the retailer's cost-cutting strategy.

Lieber, a strong supporter of the social safety net who is now assistant speaker pro-tempore of the California Assembly, is working to pass a bill that would require corporations that pay their workers poverty-level wages and fail to provide decent, affordable health insurance, to reimburse local governments for the cost of providing public assistance for those workers. Perhaps not surprisingly, Lieber's bill has attracted interest even from Republican colleagues. A campaign like this, with its antidependency rhetoric, always risks playing into the hands of those who would deprive all poor women of public assistance, but as long as it is the company that is stigmatized—not the women—it seems worth the risk. In spring 2004, that effort was on hold, pending other legislation which could render it unnecessary, including a bill, cosponsored by Lieber and Lieutenant Governor Cruz Bustamante and inspired by the grocery workers strike, that focuses particularly on health insurance for supermarket employees. Wal-Mart, which is planning to open 40 new California Supercenters in 2004, was using all its lobbying muscle to defeat that bill, claiming it infringed on "employee choice." (Lieber has also been using Wal-Mart as a poster company for her attempts to pass living wage and universal healthcare legislation.)

By the time of the 2004 presidential campaign, Wal-Mart's heinous worker-rights abuses had become so obvious that even national politicians began mentioning them. Democratic presidential hopeful John Kerry said in a speech in Newmarket, New Hampshire, "They advertise Medicaid for their workers rather than provide them absolutely with the help. I think it's disgraceful, and we need a president who's prepared to help shed light. . . . I think Wal-Mart's health-care policies are unconscionable, and the way they treat their employees is not fair." (A Wal-Mart spokeswoman, Mona Williams, wasn't happy with the candidate's comments; she denied Kerry's charges and said, "Someone better do their homework before he talks about Wal-Mart again."[35]) Howard Dean also made Wal-Mart an issue during his 2003–2004 primary campaign, saying it was important to make it easier to unionize companies like Wal-Mart. These were hopeful signs that Wal-Mart's abuses would continue to draw attention—and public rebuke—from powerful individuals.

These are encouraging developments, because they create an opening for citizens to pressure other politicians to speak out against Wal-Mart's abuses and, like Sally Lieber, attempt to craft policy solutions. Still, the complicity of both parties in Wal-Mart's power over workers points to the need for a politics that squarely challenges corporate greed, and takes the side of ordinary people.

Some of that is happening on a fragmented, local level. In the Bay Area's Contra Costa County, citizens fought for more than a year to keep Wal-Mart from building Supercenters, and tried to pass a local ordinance preventing it.

That effort attracted support from NOW, Sally Lieber's office, economic justice advocates throughout San Francisco's East Bay, the UFCW, and even Wal-Mart competitor Safeway, the union's adversary during the grocery workers' strike. Wal-Mart beat the Contra Costa ordinance in early March 2004, the same week that the grocery strike was defeated, and the first California Supercenter opened in La Quinta. But similar fights are being waged in communities nationwide. Unfortunately, Wal-Mart's opponents are not as coordinated as Wal-Mart, and they lack the retail behemoth's deep pockets. And, unlike the Christian Right, they have not yet convinced a large enough segment of the public that they are offering something better than shopping at low prices.

They will have to do that soon, because as *Dukes v. Wal-Mart* shows, Wal-Mart is a grave threat, not only to unionized workers but also to all American ideals that are at odds with profit—ideals such as justice, equality, and fairness. Wal-Mart would not have so much power if we had stronger labor laws and a more robust welfare state, and required employers to pay a living wage. The company knows that, and hires lobbyists in Washington to vigorously fight any effort at such reforms—indeed, Wal-Mart has recently beefed up this political infrastructure substantially, and it's likely that its presence in Washington will only grow more conspicuous. In 2003, the company became the top corporate donor to political candidates, making more that $1 million in contributions (two years earlier, Wal-Mart had not even ranked in the top 100). Not much will change for women like Dukes until people work together to build the kind of social and political power for workers and citizens that can balance that of Wal-Mart. That's not impossible: in Germany, unions are still so powerful that even Wal-Mart is forced to play by their rules, and pay workers a living wage.

The legal outcome of *Dukes et al. v. Wal-Mart Stores, Inc.* is of crucial importance. But its political potential could be even greater: *Dukes* could show that people are not just sheep-like consumers, but also fighters. It provides an example of people acting not only in their own interests but also on behalf of millions of complete strangers, to stand up to the world's largest company. "I feel like Norma Rae," says plaintiff Cleo Page. "I feel like we're fighting for the women. Secretly I do. When I go into Wal-Mart and I see the women working, I'm, like, 'We're fighting for you.'"

EPILOGUE

On JUNE 22, 2004, Judge Martin Jenkins certified *Betty Dukes vs. Wal-Mart Stores Inc.*, as the largest civil-rights class action in history, representing 1.6 million women. The judge called the case "historic in nature, dwarfing other employment discrimination cases that came before it." Understanding the social and political importance of his decision, Judge Jenkins observed that the year of his ruling marked the 50th anniversary of *Brown vs. Board of Education*, in which the Supreme Court ruled that the racial segregation of schools was unconstitutional. "This anniversary," he wrote, "serves as a reminder of the importance of the courts in addressing the denial of equal treatment under the law wherever and by whomever it occurs."

Addressing Wal-Mart's contention that the case would be too large and "unmanageable" to try fairly as a class action, Judge Jenkins notes that Title VII, the federal law prohibiting sex discrimination, "contains no special exception for large employers." Though the judge emphasized that he was not ruling on the "merits or probably outcome" of the case, he called the statistics presented by the plaintiffs' experts on

pay and promotion disparities at Wal-Mart "largely uncon-
tested," hardly a vote of confidence for the company's
lengthy and strenuous attempts to contest them. The judge's
ruling gave the plaintiffs almost everything they'd wanted, although he did rule that only women who had expressed interest in being promoted were entitled to compensation for
pay "lost" through discrimination in promotions. (The plaintiffs had hoped to handle this through a formula, arguing
that it was impossible to measure "interest" in a discriminatory environment.) Stephanie Odle, interviewed the night
the judge announced his decision, was ecstatic. "Now it goes
down in the history books, the largest class action ever," she
exulted, "and I started it!"

Though Wal-Mart is appealing the decision, there is no
erasing the plaintiffs' victory from history, or from the public consciousness. Every major mainstream media outlet
covered it. Newspapers put the judge's ruling on the front
page, and it was at the top of most radio and television's
hourly news reports for at least two days. The *Dallas Morning News* called Stephanie Odle the "Erin Brokovich of Wal-
Mart." Sympathy for Wal-Mart came either from right-wing
sources such as the *Wall Street Journal* editorial page (which
went far beyond Wal-Mart's own argument, not only contesting the class certification but asserting that Betty Dukes
didn't deserve to be promoted) or from mocking comedi-
ans. "If you've ever had even one woman mad at you,"
quipped one (male) radio commentator, noting that the suit
represented 1.6 million women, "you know Wal-Mart is in
trouble."

By the time the case was certified, the Dukes lawsuit had already brought about some changes at Wal-Mart.

Betty Dukes, for her part, eventually got a real raise. In 2002 she heard that two male greeters, one brand-new to the company, were earning more than she was. Wal-Mart's database, which the *Dukes v. Wal-Mart* legal team now has in its possession, confirmed the break-room gossip: the new greeter made more than $9 per hour, while Dukes's wage was $8.47. The *Dukes* lawyers filed an additional charge of sex discrimination against the company on her behalf. In March 2003, Wal-Mart gave Betty Dukes a raise, calling it an "internal equity adjustment," and she's now making over $10 an hour. It was her biggest raise in her history with the company. "They're trying to clean up," says the plaintiffs' lead counsel, Brad Seligman, and adds with a grin, "I'm sure it has absolutely nothing to do with the case!"

There's almost no doubt that Dukes wouldn't have gotten this raise without the lawsuit. She feels strongly, though, that her raise should be just the beginning of Wal-Mart's reforms. The company needs to change its treatment of all women, not just her. Besides, $10 an hour is still a lot less than Dukes would be making if she were promoted. "I'm still living far below the poverty line," she points out. "That ten dollars doesn't allow me to have my own place."

Even though it is a small raise, and less than Dukes deserves after a decade of service to the company and its customers, her raise is one of many panicked gestures Wal-Mart has made toward women since the *Dukes* plaintiffs filed suit and announced their potential class action in June 2001.

Dukes wasn't the only plaintiff or class member to see changes in her store. In early 2003, while shopping for a bra with her preteen daughter at J. C. Penney, Edith Arana ran into one of her former Wal-Mart coworkers, who had some good news. Arana had started at the Duarte store with three women who had tried for years to enter the management training program. "They would stay longer after work, because they were determined," says Arana, "but they never got that chance." Now Arana's former coworker told her, "All of a sudden, [Wal-Mart] let all three of them in. And you know what? It's because of the lawsuit." Arana is close to tears telling this story: "I said, 'When you see them, tell them I'm so happy for them.'"

Christine Kwapnoski, who has been promoted twice as a result of the lawsuit, says many women in her district who has benefited from the pressure on Wal-Mart; more than half of the people enrolled in the management training program have been female. And other women besides Dukes have received raises: Kathleen MacDonald, the candy sales clerk who was told that she made less than her male coworkers because "God made Adam first," got an 81 cent raise after an "internal review" conducted just after *Dukes* was filed—and two years after she and her coworkers began complaining about wage inequality. She was told it was neither a cost-of-living raise nor a merit raise, and—it's hard to teach old dogs new tricks—not to tell any of her coworkers!

Although it isn't likely that *Dukes* will dramatically depress Wal-Mart's stock price, over the long term (though it took a dip for a few days after Judge Jenkins announced his decision, bringing the entire Dow down with it) there's evidence that the suit is worrying shareholders, and that scares Bentonville. Before *Dukes,* the resolution introduced by the Sisters of Charity of St. Elizabeth proposing greater accountability on the promotion of women and minorities met with indifference from the Wal-Mart investors. Throughout the 1990s, about 3 to 4 percent of voting shareholders supported it—the typically lackluster showing of just about any socially conscious shareholder resolution. As the potential class-action suit gathers publicity, however, the resolution looks better and better to the nervous shareholders, 12 percent of whom voted for it at the 2003 meeting. This is considered a very high level of enthusiasm for shareholders: the same level of support for anti-apartheid resolutions in the 1980s inspired many American companies to divest in South Africa. In a surreal twist, some plaintiffs' lawyers (none of them affiliated with the firms representing *Dukes*) are considering a class-action suit against Wal-Mart on behalf of its shareholders. Their amusingly circular argument: that by discriminating against women, the company recklessly exposed its shareholders to the risk of litigation.

At the 2004 annual meeting, executives made numerous (though mostly indirect) references to the lawsuit. Betsy Reithemeyer, vice president of corporate affairs, urged employees to act as unpaid public relations officers for the company, helping Wal-Mart combat negative news coverage. "Don't let someone else define us," she said. "Tell our story better."

Wal-Mart officials are worried about what the shareholders and workers think about *Dukes*, and they are also concerned that the general public could turn against them. Even though most of their consumers will remain loyal because they need the low prices, Wal-Mart knows that public opposition could hurt them politically by stalling their efforts to expand their operations, inspiring public support for workers' unionization efforts, and mobilizing people against their antiworker lobbying efforts.

Indeed, the company's efforts at damage control have gone far beyond remedies in individual plaintiffs' stores. After the *Dukes* suit generated a flurry of negative press—which arrived on the heels of lawsuits concerning overtime, news of union organizing initiatives, a government investigation into mistreatment of immigrants, and other publicity disasters—Wal-Mart, for the first time in its history, hired an outside public relations firm to conduct "reputation research," using opinion polls and focus groups to identify problems in public perception. Board members suggested the firm Fleishman-Hillard, a company with an ethically dubious reputation of its own. A major contributor to the campaign of Los Angeles' mayor James Hahn it has drawn criticism for racking up lucrative contracts with the Los Angeles city government ever since Hahn's election.

According to a *New York Times* report, the firm found "that many people view Wal-Mart as a place of dead-end jobs, and that its performance as a corporate citizen leaves much to be desired." A Wal-Mart spokesman, Jay Allen, told the paper, "They didn't give us good marks on listening. Sometimes it was as basic as the parking lot was not clean, and that's not treating the community with respect."[2]

Clearly the report also found problems with public perception of the way women were treated, because in response to the study, new ads were created that presented Wal-Mart as a company that offers great opportunities for women. In addition to "Margaret," the district manager who said her company helps her balance family and career, ads have also featured Wal-Mart women in nontraditional jobs like trucking (of course, like most companies, Wal-Mart has few female truckers). Allen said it was the consultant's research rather than the lawsuit that prompted the ads, though it's obvious that the lawsuit, as well as public criticism on other issues, prompted the research.[3]

Wal-Mart is ambiguous about whether its public relations efforts are intended to correct a false impression, or intended to highlight the company's attempt to correct acknowledged bad behavior. Wal-Mart has repeatedly denied discriminating against women, but Allen told the *Times*, with surprising frankness, "We would acknowledge that we need to get better as an employer. The lawsuit has certainly heightened our awareness of that." He said the company would be making some changes, but then he qualified that statement and echoed what other Wal-Mart officials have said about *Dukes v. Wal-Mart*: "At the same time, we can't change who we are. We can't change what makes Wal-Mart, Wal-Mart."[4]

Along with the marketing blitz, the company did institute some genuine reforms. It started a small-scale program called Leadership Express to train qualified new managers (men and women) more quickly, which seemed to be an implicit acknowledgment that many people were not getting the promotions they deserve. The program started in early 2003, and at the June shareholders' meeting of that year, Charlyn Jarrells-Porter, then the senior vice president of the People Division, was able to announce that participation in the Leadership Express program was 50 percent female and 25 percent minority. (She also said "more than ninety people" had been promoted through the program, a small number given the size of Wal-Mart.) Job posting has improved substantially. Since January 2003, presumably as a result of *Dukes*, the company has been posting nearly all jobs at least within the store, and posting nationwide for openings in management training.

In January 2004, the company also instituted a formal system making it easier for workers to apply for the management training program through the company's employee computer network, rather than depending on their manager's recommendation. (Wal-Mart describes this as an "enhancement" to a practice already in place, but plaintiffs' lawyers say they had no knowledge of it, despite extensive discovery concerning the company's hiring practices.)

In early 2004, Wal-Mart announced it was creating a department to oversee diversity, including women's issues, and a new position, chief diversity officer, to be filled by Jarrells-Porter. The creation of this position was one of many reforms sought by the *Dukes* plaintiffs, who see it as a major step toward improving the company's policies.

The company has also increased its number of high-ranking women. Of the four women among Wal-Mart's 24 senior officers, 3 may owe their jobs to Dukes—a greeter who still doesn't earn a living wage. Claire Watts became a senior vice president of merchandising in October 2001 and was promoted to her current position, executive vice president for merchandising, in 2003. Linda Dillman became senior vice president and chief information officer of Wal-Mart in 2002 and, like Watts, was promoted to executive vice president in 2003. M. Susan Chambers was named senior vice president of benefits and insurance administration in January 2002 and has since been promoted to executive vice president of risk management. (The fourth senior officer, Celia Swanson, executive vice president of membership and marketing and administration for Sam's Club, has been in her position since December 2000, before the suit was filed.) In a short time, Wal-Mart has impressively improved the sex ratio in its top executive ranks, and now it's about average for corporate America: in 2002, women represented 15.7 percent of top officers in the nation's 500 largest companies.[5]

The two women on Wal-Mart's 14-member board probably owe their seats to Dukes as well. Two months after *Dukes* was filed, Wal-Mart appointed Dawn Lepore, a vice president and the chief information officer at Charles Schwab, to its board of directors. (Betsy Sanders, who'd replaced Hillary Clinton in 1993, had left a few years earlier.) In June 2003, Lepore was joined by M. Michelle Burns, formerly a partner at Arthur Andersen and now executive vice president and chief financial officer of Delta Air Lines. Though 2 out of 14 may sound like a low number, unfortunately it isn't that bad, compared to many other large companies: 67 of the Fortune 500 boards are 100 percent male.

Perhaps most significantly, at the 2004 shareholders' meeting, just a few weeks before the judge announced his decision to certify the *Dukes* case, Wal-Mart announced that it was restructuring its wage system to make it more equitable. Under the new system, assured CEO Lee Scott, no workers' wages would be decreased, but some would receive raises. The same day, also at the shareholders' meeting, Scott announced a new plan to tie managers' pay to their success in meeting goals for the promotion of women. During the discovery phase of *Dukes*, Jeff Reeves, a former Sam's Club People Division vice president, had testified that without such incentives, rhetoric from Wal-Mart about improving the status of women would be nothing by "lip service."

Though all the plaintiffs and class members feel strongly that changing Wal-Mart has been worth their effort, the gains have not been without cost for some of them. Many have sacrificed friendships with Wal-Mart coworkers. Management retaliated against Micki Earwood by conducting a smear campaign against her within the store, charging, among other things, that she'd broken the confidentiality obligations of her job and discussed employees' wages with other coworkers. She denies the charge, yet it had an effect: "People who had been my colleagues and friends for almost twelve years were told lies about me by store managers," she says. Many former coworkers were afraid they'd lose their jobs if they talked to her. Recently, Earwood ran into a former coworker at the mall. They talked, but the woman kept looking around nervously, afraid to be seen speaking with Earwood.

The lawsuit also has created tensions within some families; since Wal-Mart is the largest private employer in the United States, many of the women involved have relatives and other intimates who work for the company. Farroukh Moinian, Stephanie Odle's boyfriend and the father of her child, works for Sam's Club as a store manager. (They met in 1993, when both were working at the Vacaville Sam's Club, where Moinian was a store manager. Their child was born in November of that year, and now they own a house together.) They have had disagreements about *Dukes*, but he's as supportive as he probably could be under the circumstances. "I don't expect him to be right behind me at every press conference," she explains, "because this is his company, but I'm happy to say that he lets me stand up for what I believe in and doesn't give me any grief for it. He's like, 'You know what? All you're doing is fighting for your rights, and that's okay. I support you on that. Just keep me out of it.'

"I just don't want to bring him into it," she says, "and I don't think he wants to know [details]. I don't want to mess. . . up [his job] for him.

"It's really awkward," she admits. "We really just don't talk about [the lawsuit]." When Odle flew to New York to appear on the *Today* show in connection with the case, she didn't tell Moinian until the day before she left.

As admirably as they handle the situation, however, the case has created a rift between the couple, much of it unspoken. "You know he just wants to vent, and I just want to vent," she says. "But I just find my mother to vent to, and he's got his friends that he vents to about it, I'm sure." Ultimately, though, Odle empathizes with Moinian's dedication to Sam's Club. "Sam's was my life, and I understand that it's his life. I understand that he is Wal-Mart-ized like I was."

Many plaintiffs and witnesses who are no longer working at Wal-Mart are still having trouble finding new jobs. Some of this has to do with a slow economy or living in regions where jobs are scarce even in good times. Earwood wonders whether the lawsuit is hurting her chances to find employment. "You know, you have an outstanding interview and everything goes well, and they were gonna call your references, and you never hear from them again. And you have to wonder . . ." But she says, too, that since her Wal-Mart experience, she's now much more cautious in looking for an employer. "It changes you, you know? I don't know if I can ever work for a big corporation again."

In fact, employers are often afraid of workers who are plaintiffs in class-action suits. Odle has encountered retaliation from subsequent employers. In March 2000, she got a job as an assistant manager at the retailer Old Navy, in Norman, Oklahoma. After the *Dukes* plaintiffs held a press conference in California in June 2001 announcing the suit, the *Norman Transcript* ran a story about it with her photo. Back at Old Navy, says Odle, "My boss lost her mind. She called me a bunch of names, in front of hourly employees," and then called the district manager asking to fire Odle. Odle promptly went out and found a job at Lowe's, a home improvement chain store, and then handed in her resignation to the district manager, who was in turn furious with the store manager. To his credit, he insisted that Odle stay on the job, assuring her, "What you do with Wal-Mart is none of our business."

After three years at Old Navy, Odle was recruited by another clothing retailer, Aeropostale. Odle again said nothing to her bosses about the case, but when her Aeropostale supervisor turned on the TV and saw her new employee on the *Today* show, she wasn't pleased. When Odle came to work, her supervisor greeted her with a curt, "We need to talk." She was upset that Odle had not mentioned the class action suit when she was hired, and angry at Odle for telling the *Today* show that if the plaintiffs won and Wal-Mart offered her a job, she would take it. Odle laughs at that: "And I said, 'Well, as of yet, they haven't offered me my job back, so I don't really think there's anything we need to talk about.'" That conversation was only the beginning of what turned into regular harassment. Odle's boss wrote her up constantly for invented infractions, until Odle finally couldn't take it and quit. "You find another job and you have to go through it again and again," she says and sighs. "Just because you're trying to fight for your constitutional rights and make a change, make a difference! You'd think people would be like, 'You go!' But instead you're labeled a troublemaker."

Despite the uneven record of class actions in changing institutions, the plaintiffs, witnesses, and lawyers involved in *Dukes v. Wal-Mart* are in accord that transforming Wal-Mart is their goal. Joyce Moody, the witness who is now organizing Wal-Mart workers for the United Food and Commercial Workers Union, says she is not involved in the lawsuit for the money. Of a cash settlement she says, "If it comes, it comes. If it don't, it don't. That, I'm not worried about. I just want to make [the company] a better place for women, who comprise most of the workers at Wal-Mart."

Seligman agrees: "We will not have done our job unless we change Wal-Mart."

In addition to damages "commensurate with the Defendant's ability to pay and to deter future conduct"—which any court would be highly unlikely to award in Wal-Mart's case—the plaintiffs are asking that all class members be restored to the positions they would hold at Wal-Mart and be paid the wages they would earn "but for Defendant's discriminatory practices." In other words, they are asking that all women should get the pay and promotions they deserve, a potentially massive administrative task, but an inspiring one.

If the plaintiffs are successful, the size of the company will present a challenge for those devising broader reforms. Joe Sellers notes that no class-action suit has ever attempted institutional change on this scale. Payout of money to the class members would be "the easy part. The hard part is how you change the corporate culture. And we have been struggling with that. There's no simple way of doing it." Sellers, one of the plaintiffs' co-counsels, is the attorney most involved in this task, which is appropriate in light of his years of public- policy experience. Wal-Mart's size makes it almost more comparable to a government than a company, so changing it is clearly a task for a policy maker.

Many of the workers interviewed for this book have mentioned that they would like to see on-site day-care centers at the stores, as Target has in a few of its corporate offices. It seems unlikely that a judge would view this as a direct remedy for the problems enumerated in *Dukes*, but there is no doubt that it would change the status of women at Wal-Mart and transform the corporate culture.

A settlement—if there is a settlement—would probably set specific goals for the promotion of women into Wal-Mart management.

Judge Jenkin's decision meant that the suit would probably continue to bring about reforms. During the year leading up to the certification hearing in September 2003, the two legal teams had, at Wal-Mart's request, met and discussed settlement possibilities. Wal-Mart's lawyers were open to imposing some institutional reforms on their client: "It's time to bring this company into the twenty-first century," declared Wal-Mart's lead defense counsel, Nancy Abell. But the parties couldn't agree on specific changes. They will probably continue to struggle to find a common ground, but now, the plaintiffs may have the upper hand.

Stephanie Odle thinks *Dukes* is changing the company, is prompting it to make progress in promoting women, but she now looks at the company from a far more sober perspective than earlier: "I'm sad that it took this for them to open their eyes. I think that they have a long way to go. They're making steps in the right direction, but I wish they were doing it because it was the right thing to do, instead of doing it because they have to."

Betty Dukes is happy to be speaking on behalf of Wal-Mart's women, and is glad that the suit can do what one person cannot, despite the company's insistence that workers "can speak for themselves." "There was a lot of women in

my store that felt"— Dukes pauses and searches for exactly
the right word—"disenfranchised. Like I did. But who are
you to stand up? You are just a little dog, and they got a
dozen pit bulls." Sitting in Seligman's office after all the
lawyers have gone home, she catches a glimpse of her name
on a legal brief and starts. *"Betty Dukes versus Wal-Mart Stores,"*
she says as she shakes her head in amazement. Even now,
she says, "It hasn't quite sunk in."

Dukes looks forward to following the suit's progress. At
times before joining the lawsuit, she despaired of changing
Wal-Mart, but now she is optimistic about where things
might lead. "Now I'm in federal court," she pronounced
with satisfaction, as if she were making a speech, though we
are just sitting on a park bench. "And the lawsuit is in my
name. And now they are spending millions of dollars defending themselves. . . . We, the women of Wal-Mart, will
have our day in court. . . . They will answer our charges: that
they have treated us unfairly and we deserved better. Because
we are the backbone of their company, and we have made
them wealthy. We have made them *wealthy*."

Notes

Introduction

1. Unless otherwise specified, quotations come from interviews conducted by the author. Use of the word "testified" indicates statements made in depositions or affidavits.

2. Bob Ortega, *In Sam We Trust: The Untold Story of Sam Walton and Wal-Mart, the World's Most Powerful Retailer* (New York: Three Rivers, 2000), p. xviii.

3. Peter S. Goodman and Philip P. Pan, "Chinese Workers Pay for Wal-Mart's Low Prices," *Washington Post,* February 8, 2004, p. A1.

4. "Wal-Mart to Convene Meeting in China," Xinhua News Service, March 4, 2004.

Chapter 1

1. Gay Jervey, "Runaway Train," *American Lawyer,* July–August 1992, p. 58.

2. Chuck Salter, "The Next Big (Legal) Thing?" *Fast Company,* April 2003, p. 112.

3. Impact Fund, *Tenth Anniversary Annual Report* (Berkeley, Calif.: Impact Fund, 2003), p. 3.

4. Marc Bendick, "The Representation of Women Among Managers at Wal-Mart: A Preliminary Analysis Based on EEO-1 Data" (June 2001). Unpublished.

5. Sam Walton with John Huey, *Made in America: My Story* (New York: Bantam, 1992), pp. 217–18.

6. Walton, though a moderate conservative, seems to have been proud of his politically independent wife, writing, "One of the reasons I fell for Helen in the first place was that she was her own woman. . . . Some of her causes aren't all that popular with some of these fairly extreme groups. But I'll tell you this: she doesn't ask me what she should think, and I'd be the last person on earth to try to tell her" (Walton and Huey, *Made in America,* pp. 96–97).

7. Bob Ortega, *In Sam We Trust: The Untold Story of Sam Walton and Wal-Mart, the World's Most Powerful Retailer* (New York: Three Rivers, 2000), p. 211.

8. Ibid.

9. Ibid., pp. 212–13.

10. Board duties at major companies take up about a dozen hours per year, which means that, although Clinton's payment was not exorbitant for the director of a major corporation, her hourly rate was about 156 times that of a female Wal-Mart worker.

11. Ibid.

12. Ibid., pp. 214–15.

13. Cora Daniels, "Women vs. Wal-Mart," *Fortune*, July 21, 2003, p. 80.

Chapter 2

1. Sam Walton with John Huey, *Made in America: My Story*, (New York: Bantam, 1992), p. 23.

2. Ibid., p. 98.

3. Constance L. Hays, "In Wal-Marts Close to Bases, Emotions Spill into the Aisle," *New York Times*, p. A1.

4. The *Dukes* class-certification brief lists the reference to "girls" as evidence of the sexist atmosphere at Wal-Mart. Many women refer to themselves and to each other as girls, regardless of their real age. Doubtless many of the women working in the stores would not have been offended at the term "girls"; however, "Janie-Q" fails even the most indulgent measure of human dignity.

5. Mary Williams Walsh, "So Where Are the Corporate Husbands?" *New York Times*, June 24, 2001, p. C1.

Chapter 3

1. Gray and his firm, Jones, Day, Reavis & Pogue, are no longer working on this case.

2. Richard Drogin, "Statistical Analysis of Gender Patterns in Wal-Mart Workforce," February 2003, p. 17, available at http://www.walmartclass.com/walmartclass94.pl?wsi=0&websys_screen=all_reports_view&websys_id=18.

3. Marc Bendick, "The Representation of Women in Store Management at Wal-Mart Stores, Inc.," January 2003, available at http://www.walmartclass.com/walmartclass94.pl?wsi=0&websys_screen=all_reports_view&websys_id=20.

4. Ibid.

5. Drogin, "Statistical Analysis of Gender Patterns in Wal-Mart Workforce," p. 5.

6. Reed Abelson, "6 Women Sue Wal-Mart, Charging Job and Promotion Bias," *New York Times*, June 20, 2001, p. C1.

Chapter 4

1. Richard Drogin, "Statistical Analysis of Gender Patterns in Wal-Mart Workforce," p. 44, available at http://www.walmartclass.com/walmartclass94.pl?wsi =0&websys_screen=all_reports_view&websys_id=18.

2. In the retail industry as a whole, 75 percent of cashiers are women. The industry-wide pay gap between male and female year-round full-time cashiers is about the same as Wal-Mart's (U.S. Department of Labor, Bureau of Labor Statistics, "Highlights of Women's Earnings 2002," report 972, September 2003, p. 12, available at http://www.bls.gov/cps/cpswom2002.pdf).

3. Drogin, "Statistical Analysis of Gender Patterns in Wal-Mart Workforce," p. 17.

4. Abell's was the third firm Wal-Mart hired on the *Dukes* case—in fact, the lawyers defending Wal-Mart had a higher turnover rate than the company's cashiers. The company has been tight-lipped about the reasons for the revolving door, but relationships with the first two firms are said to have faltered partly on account of Wal-Mart's famous tightfistedness (lawyers don't like being underpaid any better than greeters do). It's just as likely that Wal-Mart was surprised and dismayed by the strength of the plaintiffs' emerging case, and needed bigger and better guns: the firm now representing them, Paul, Hastings, Janofsky & Walker, of San Francisco, is one of the premier corporate defenders in California and is famous for "cleanup" work—repairing cases that have been poorly litigated.

5. National Labor Relations Board, "Wal-Mart Stores, Case 18–CA–14757," *Decisions of the National Labor Relations Board,* September 17, 2003, p. 6, available at http://www.nlrb.gov/nlrb/shared_files/decisions/340/340-31.pdf.

6. Philip Kellerman, Letters to the Editor, *The Nation,* Febuary 24, 2003.

7. House of Representatives, Committee on Education and the Workforce, "Everyday Low Wages: The Hidden Price We All Pay for Wal-Mart," staff report, February 16, 2004, p. 5, available at http://edworkforce.house.gov/ democrats/WALMARTREPORT.pdf.

8. Quoted in Philippa Dunne and Doug Henwood, "Decent Sales Tax Receipts, but Discounting a Worry," *The Liscio Report on the Economy,* on-line newsletter, December 10, 2003, p. 2.

9. AFL-CIO, "Wal-Mart: An Example of Why Workers Remain Uninsured and Underinsured," report, October 2003, p. 14, available at http://www. aflcio.org/issuespolitics/healthpolicy/ upload/Wal-Mart_final.pdf.

10. Ibid., citing Kaiser Family Foundation and Health Research and Educational Trust, "Employer Health Benefits: 2003 Annual Survey," report, p. 75, original available at http://www.kff.org/insurance/ehbs2003-1-set.cfm.

11. Andy Miller, "Wal-Mart Stands Out on Rolls of Peachcare," *Atlanta Journal-Constitution,* February 27, 2004.

12. Rebecca Cook, "Lawmakers Blast Business for Sponging off State Health Care," Associated Press, state and local wire, February 27, 2003.

13. National Committee on Pay Equity, "Questions and Answers on Pay Equity," available at http://www.pay-equity.org/info-Q&A.html.

14. Center for the Advancement of Women, "Progress and Perils: New Agenda for Women," report, June 2003, p. 11, available at http://www.advance-women.org/womens_research/Progress&Perils.pdf.

15. Ibid., p. 14.

16. U.S. Department of Labor, Bureau of Labor Statistics, "Women's Earnings 2002," pp. 11–14.

Chapter 5

1. Sam Walton with John Huey, *Made in America: My Story*, (New York: Bantam, 1992), p. 217.

2. "Best Companies for Latinas to Work for in the U.S.," *Latina Style*, http://www.latinastyle.com/2001list.html.

3. Vicki Schultz, "Telling Stories About Women and Work: Judicial Interpretations of Sex Segregation in the Workplace in Title VII Cases Raising the Lack of Interest Argument," *Harvard Law Review*, June 1990 (discussing *EEOC v. Sears, Roebuck & Co.,* 839 F.2d 302, 311 [7th Cir. 1988]).

4. Ibid.

5. Reed Abelson, "Anti-Bias Agency Is Short on Will and Cash," *New York Times,* July 1, 2001, p. C1.

6. Schultz, "Telling Stories About Women and Work."

7. Arthur M. Louis, "Settlement Detailed in Lucky Suit," *San Francisco Chronicle,* December 17, 1993, p. D1.

8. Ibid.

9. "Employees of a Megastore Get the Power of Numbers," *New York Times,* January 12, 1997, p. A14.

10. Michael Selmi, "The Price of Discrimination: The Nature of Class Action Employment Discrimination Litigation and Its Effects," *Texas Law Review,* April 2003.

11. Ibid.

12. Ibid.

13. Ibid.

14. Ibid.

15. Alan Huffman, *Mississippi in Africa: The Saga of the Slaves of Prospect Hill Plantation and Their Legacy in Liberia Today* (New York: Gotham, 2004), p. 17.

16. Impact Fund, *Tenth Anniversary Annual Report* (Berkeley, Calif.: Impact Fund, 2003), p. 4.

17. Theodore Eisenberg and Geoffrey P. Miller, "Attorneys' Fees in Class Action Settlements: An Empirical Study," New York University Center for Law and Business Research, Working Paper Series, paper CLB-03-017, September 24, 2003, available at http://www.stern.nyu.edu/clb/WP2003/03-017.pdf.

18. Thomas Kochan et al., "The Effects of Diversity on Business Performance: Report of the Diversity Business Network," *Human Resource Management*

42, no. 1 (October 2002): 3–21 (available at http://www.shrm.org/foundation/Kochan03HRMJ.pdf).

19. Fay Hansen, "Diversity's Business Case Doesn't Add Up," *Workforce Management,* April 2003, p. 28.

Chapter 6

1. Richard Drogin, "Statistical Analysis of Gender Patterns in Wal-Mart Workforce," February 2003, p. 17, available at http://www.walmartclass.com/walmartclass94.pl?wsi=0&websys_screen=all_reports_view&websys_id=18.

2. Vicky Lovell, Xue Song, and April Shaw, "The Benefits of Unionization for Workers in the Retail Food Industry," report (Washington, D.C.: Institute for Women's Policy Research, 2002; available at http://www.iwpr.org/pdf/c352.pdf). The study was funded by the United Food and Commercial Workers (UFCW), which is obviously not an objective player. Still, the IWPR is a reputable research institution. Asked about the UFCW relationship, Vicky Lovell, the lead author of the report, says the union funding did limit the scope of the research. She wanted to compare unionized and nonunionized women for specific poverty indicators, for example, and the UFCW was not interested in doing that. But Lovell said the union did not manipulate the data, or influence her interpretation of her research. In any case, older studies conducted by academic researchers have reached similar conclusions.

3. John Dicker, "Union Blues at Wal-Mart," *The Nation,* July 8, 2002.

Chapter 7

1. Wendy Liebmann, "How America Shops: I Shop, Therefore I Am," address to the Global Health and Beauty Expo, New York City, June 21, 2000.

2. Ibid.

3. Joanne Thomas Yaccato, "Special Report: Reaching Women," *Strategy* (Brunico Communications), November 18, 2002, p. 19.

4. Michael Bitman et al., "When Does Gender Trump Money?" Institute for Policy Research Working Paper 02–34 (Evanston, Ill.: Institute for Policy Research, Fall 2002). Most studies on how much time people spend on household labor are controversial, because it is so hard to measure, but there is little doubt that women still do considerably more of it than men.

5. Joanne Yaccato, *The 80% Minority: Reaching the Real World of Women Consumers* (Toronto: Viking Canada, 2003). Yaccato's work focuses on Canada, but American sources agree on the 80 percent figure.

6. LouAnn Lofton, "Supermarket Smackdown," *The Motley Fool,* April 3, 2003.

7. *Women's Wear Daily,* "Let's Talk Shop: Survey Finds Out What Factors Influence Apparel Purchases," *Cleveland Plain Dealer,* January 21, 1999, p. 1F.

8. Anne D'Innocenzio, "At Sweet 16, Mary-Kate and Ashley Olsen Expand a Billion-Dollar Brand," Associated Press, June 17, 2002.

9. Recent reports have suggested that Mary-Kate is in rehab, and the twins are "growing apart" and may split up the business partnership. It will be interesting to see if Wal-Mart can handle them as their image becomes more complex.

10. Alissa Quart, *Branded: The Buying and Selling of Teenagers* (New York: Perseus Books, 2003), p. xiii.

11. Centers of Disease Control and Prevention, National Center for Health Statistics, "Health, United States," report (Atlanta: Centers for Disease Control, 2002), table 70, available at http://www.cdc.gov/nchs/products/pubs/pudb/hestats/obese/obese99.htm.

12. Tannette Johnson, "Full-figuring It Out," *Milwaukee Journal Sentinel,* April 2, 2003, p. 1D.

13. Michele Weston, Venus Diva website, http://www.venusimaging.com.

14. Ruth La Ferla, "Front Row," *New York Times,* May 13, 2003, p. B11.

15. "From Plus-Sized to Curvaceous," http://www.fashionwindows.com/fashion/2003/curvation.asp.

16. U.S. Surgeon General, "The Facts About Overweight and Obesity at a Glance," available at http://www.surgeongeneral.gov/topics/obesity/calltoaction/fact_glance.htm.

17. Information Resources, Inc., "Wal-Mart Update: Supersizing the Supermarket," *Times & Trends,* October 2003.

18. Andrew W. Franklin, "The Impact of Wal-Mart Supercenters on Supermarket Concentration in U.S. Metropolitan Areas," *Agribusiness,* 17, no. 1 (2001): 105–14.

19. Chris Reidy and Kathy McCabe, "In Tight Times, Value Is a Big Draw," *Boston Globe,* December 4, 2001, p. C1.

20. Lou Hirsh, "Research Shows Who Shops at Target and Wal-Mart," *The Desert Sun,* March 28, 2004, citing a study by Bob Martels, a St. Louis consultant.

21. Neil Buckley, "Wal-Mart to Move into Financial Services," *Financial Times,* January 8, 2003, p. 21.

22. Mark Husson, "Wal-Mart Food: Uneven Share Gain Continues," report (New York: Merrill-Lynch, 2002), p. 6.

23. Wendy Zellner, "No Way to Treat a Lady," *Business Week,* March 3, 2003, p. 63.

24. Cindy Kay, "Wise Up," Letters to the Editor, *Winona Post,* July 23, 2003.

25. Carolyn Goree, "Wal-Mart," Letters to the Editor, *Winona Post,* July 30, 2003.

26. Sara Jennings, "Wal-Mart a Help to Seniors," *Winona Post,* July 23, 2003.

27. MMR (Mass Market Retailers), "Supers v Wal-Mart," http://www.massmarketretailers.com/articles/Supers_vs_Walmart.html.

28. Hirsh, "Research Shows Who Shops at Target and Wal-Mart."

29. Husson, "Wal-Mart Food," p. 6.

30. "Campaign Succeeding Against Sexy Magazine Covers at Checkouts," *AFA Journal* (American Family Association), May 2001, available at http://www.afa.net/journal/may/activisma.asp.

31. Husson, "Wal-Mart Food," p. 6.

32. Stuart Ewen, *Captains of Consciousness: Advertising and the Social Roots of the Consumer Culture* (New York: McGraw-Hill, 1976), p. 26.

33. Ibid., p. 43.

34. Lizabeth Cohen, *A Consumer's Republic: The Politics of Mass Consumption in Postwar America* (New York: Vintage, 2003).

35. Holly Ramer, "Kerry Blasts Wal-Mart Policies," Associated Press, October 10, 2003, p. A5.

Epilogue

1. "Wal-Mart Asks Workers to 'Tell Our Story,'" Emily Kaiser, Reuters, June 4, 2004.

2. Constance L. Hays, "Wal-Mart, Aware Its Image Suffers, Studies Repairs," *New York Times,* August 14, 2003, p. C1.

3. Ibid.

4. Ibid.

5. "Catalyst Marks Gains in Numbers of Women in Corporate Officers in America's Top 500 Companies," Catalyst (an organization promoting women's advancement in corporate America), press release, November 19, 2002.

Acknowledgments

Many women—some named in the book, others un-named—generously shared their Wal-Mart experiences with me. Without their trust, good faith, and insight, I could not have written this book. I especially thank Betty Dukes. My gratitude also to the plaintiffs' lawyers—who spent many hours helping me understand the case and allowed me access to their clients—with a special thanks to Debra Smith. I'm also very grateful to Deb Schwartz, Mary Broughton, and Ingrid Tischer.

Without Vanessa Mobley, the book's first editor, *Selling Women Short* simply would not have come to pass. Her continued enthusiasm for the project has been inspiring. My agent, Faye Bender, has been an author's dream, providing feedback, encouragement, and advice far exceeding her obligations. My second editor, Jo Ann Miller, improved the book tremendously with her careful editing and deeply intelligent suggestions. Big thanks as well to Ellen Garrison, Liz Maguire, and Doris Michaels.

I would like to thank the Fund for Investigative Journalism and the Dick Goldensohn Fund for their generous financial support; Barbara Ehrenreich for writing *Nickel and Dimed*, which was a great inspiration to me; Matt Driggs and Laura Starecheski, without whom I would never have finished on time; Heather Rogers for our "book group" of two—I already miss our meetings, which were absolutely critical; John Stamm for his incredible generosity in the pursuit of photo perfection; and Betsy Reed, my *Nation* magazine editor, for publishing my cover story on Wal-Mart and for providing this book's title. Thanks too: Tai Moses and Don Hazen of Alternet, Corinna Barnard of Women's E-news, and Alleen Barber of *Newsday* for publishing material that, in some form, ended up in this book.

Each for distinct reasons, I'm grateful to Jennifer Berkshire, Heather Boushey, Randall Dodd, Deb Figart, Laura Flanders, Emily Gordon, Kate Gordon, Caryn Gorden, Casey Greenfield, Caledonia Kearns, Dan Lazare, Lisa Levy, Karen Miller, Gina Neff, Susan Phillips, Christian Parenti, Joel Schalit, Anya Schiffrin, Courtney Utt, Katrina vanden Heuvel, Al Zack, and Wendy Zeitz. Huge thank-yous to my wonderful parents, Jay and Helen Featherstone, and sisters, Caitlin and Miranda.

My deepest love and gratitude to my husband, Doug Henwood, who helped with this book in so many ways and makes my life so profoundly delightful. What a lucky woman I am.

Index